Introduction

The Focke-Wulf Fw 190 was arguably the Luftwaffe's most outstanding piston-engined fighter of World War Two, virtually dominating the skies over Europe for more than a year after its initial introduction into service in the summer of 1941. Continual development and improvements then kept it at the forefront of operations in the theatres of Northern Europe, the Mediterranean and the Eastern Front for the remainder of the war while maintaining a competitive edge over many other types as well as gaining and retaining the grudging respect of Allied and Soviet pilots.

Despite being designed as a Fighter, the BMW 801-engined Fw 190 sub-types performed practically every role possible for a single-engined, single-seat aircraft – including offensive and defensive day fighter, day and night fighter-bomber, ground attack, reconnaissance platform, night-fighter and trainer.

The Fw 190A also served in the Hungarian Air Force during the later stages of World War Two, the Turkish Air Force from mid-1942 to 1948, and post-war with the French where the SNCAC aircraft company re-built over fifty Fw 190A-5/A-6s under the designation NC 900 for service with the new Armée de l'Air.

Despite having standard factory-applied camouflage and markings schemes, many Fw 190s were also finished in a variety of 'on unit' and 'seasonal' and/or operational theatre' schemes which add to the aircraft's story.

Martin Derry & Neil Robinson

Opposite page:
A factory-fresh Fw 190A-5/U3 Jabo fighter still with its factory codes, GL+MY, in place. Fitted with an ETC 501 centreline rack for drop tanks or bombs, its only fixed armament consisted of just two MG 151 cannon.

Below:
An early Fw 190A, possibly an A-3 or A-4, of I./JG 54, being run-up on a snow-covered Russian airfield in the winter of 1942-43. Note the temporary white 'snow' upper surface camouflage, I./JG 54's shield and the arms of the City of Nuremberg on the cowling.

Acknowledgements
The authors would like to thank the following for their help and generous assistance in the compilation of this book. Namely, Tom Ketley (of the Barry Ketley Collection), Neil Page, Steve Page, Mark Rolfe and Carl Vincent, with special thanks extended to Martin Mace for his support and encouragement throughout this project, and also to Chris Goss who supplied photographs that proved essential for the ordnance section.

Note regarding photo sources:
NARA = National Archives and Records Administration.
NMD = National Museum of Denmark
SA-kuva = Finnish Wartime Photographic Archive.
HMP = Historic Military Press
USNHHC = US Navy Naval History and Heritage Command
Unless otherwise stated all remaining photos are provided via the authors.

Design, development & prototypes

Top right:
Kurt Tank, the brilliant German aeronautical engineer and test pilot who led the design department at Focke-Wulf from 1931 to 1945, photographed in 1941. Responsible for designing several important Luftwaffe aircraft, (including the Fw 200 Condor), he is perhaps most famously remembered for the Fw 190, of which over 20,000 were produced from 1941 to 1945. In January 1943, he was named honorary professor with a chair at the Technical University of Braunschweig, in recognition of his work developing aircraft and in 1944 the Reichsluftfahrtministerium (German Air Ministry) decided that new fighter aircraft designations must include the chief designer's name. Kurt Tank's new designs were therefore given the prefix Ta, his most notable late-war design being the high-speed/high-altitude Ta 152 single-engine fighter, a continuation of the Fw 190 lineage.

Below right:
Kurt Tank with Oberstleutnant Adolph Galland, possibly photographed in the autumn of 1941 when Galland was Geschwader Kommodore of JG 26, and II./JG 26 was re-equipping with Fw 190A-1s. At the time, the rest of JG 26 was being re-equipped with the then new Bf 109F. Of note is the Messerschmitt Bf 108 in the background.

As a result of an *Reichsluftfahrtministerium* (RLM – Reich Air Ministry) request in autumn 1937 for an alternative to the Messerschmitt Bf 109, then Germany's frontline fighter, Dipl Ing Kurt Tank offered a number of suggestions, mostly incorporating liquid-cooled inline engines. However, it was not until his design utilizing an air-cooled 14-cylinder radial engine emerged that the RLM's interest was aroused, especially because a radial engine would not affect production of the Bf 109's Daimler-Benz inline engine.

The first prototype **Fw 190 V1** (D-OPZE) was powered by a 1,529hp BMW 139 14-cylinder, two-row, radial engine and first flew on 1 June 1939. It immediately showed its pedigree, with good handling qualities, good all round visibility and impressive speed – initially around 610km/h (379mph). Another feature was its stable, widely spaced undercarriage, ideal for operating from primitive airfields which allowed the Fw 190 to operate more safely and suffer fewer accidents than the Messerschmitt Bf 109 with its closely spaced landing gear. However, the location of the cockpit directly behind the engine, resulted in it becoming uncomfortably hot. During the first flight the temperature reached 55°C (131°F), which led Focke-Wulf's chief test pilot, Hans Sander to comment that "It was like sitting with both feet in the fireplace."

Further flight tests resulted in a smaller diameter spinner cap being fitted that only covered the hub of the three-bladed VDM propeller in order to increase airflow. In an attempt to further increase airflow over the tightly-cowled engine, a 10-blade cooling fan installed in front of the engine's reduction gear housing (later replaced by a 12-blade fan) was fitted at the front opening of the redesigned cowling and geared to be

Design, development & prototypes

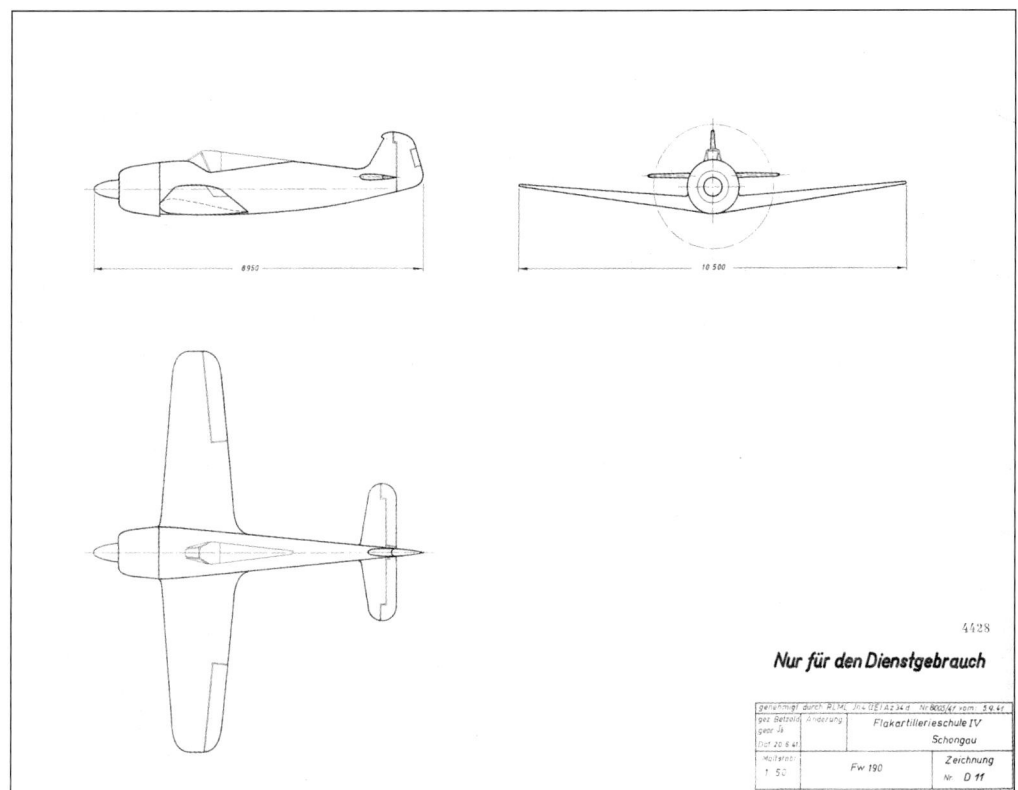

Left:
Basic general arrangement drawings of the Fw 190 that appears to have been allocated to Flakartillerieschule IV (Anti-aircraft Artillery Training School IV), at Schongau, as an aircraft recognition poster when the type entered Luftwaffe service.

Below:
The Fw 190 V5, still fitted with the original small wing which was tapered in plan and was designated V5k (for kleine fläche) to differentiate it from when it was later fitted with a new wing following a collision with a vehicle in August 1940 that sent it back to the factory for major repairs. On completion it reappeared with a longer span and larger wing now designated V5g for grosse fläche (large wing).

driven at 3.12 times engine speed. This quickly became standard on the Fw 190 and nearly all the other German aircraft powered by the BMW 801 (destined to replace the BMW 139). The V1 flew in this form on 1 December 1939 having had Luftwaffe national markings applied as well as the *stammkennzeichen* (factory code) RM+CA.

The **Fw 190 V2** FL+OZ (later RM+CB) first flew on 31 October 1939 and was equipped from the outset with the new spinner and cooling fan. It was armed with two Rheinmetall-Borsig 7.92mm (.312in) MG 17 machine guns, one in each wing root. Small tabs were fitted to all control surfaces and adjusted on the ground after the initial test flights to compensate for the wide tolerances typical in mass-produced aircraft. However, the elevators were the only control surfaces that needed to be trimmed in flight, achieved using an all-moving tailplane that was electrically adjustable from a -3º to a +5º angle of

Above:
Line-up of prototype airframes including one of the pre-production series Fw 190A-0s with factory codes (stammkennzeichen) KB+PC.

Right:
An early Fw 190A-1, werknummer 067, (with the standard asymmetrical teardrop cowling bulges), still with its factory codes TI+DQ in place. Delivered to II./JG 26 in late summer 1941, it was subsequently issued to 4 Staffel. Note the inner mainwheel doors open and hanging vertically down and the thin black outline to the swastika on the fin.

incidence. The tailplane featured relatively small horizontal and vertical surfaces, and the rudder and elevators, like the ailerons, only had ground-adjustable tabs.

Another aspect of the new design was the extensive use of electrically-powered equipment instead of hydraulic systems (used by most aircraft manufacturers of the time). On the first two prototypes the main undercarriage was hydraulic but starting with the third prototype the undercarriage was operated by electric motors in the wings, controlled from the cockpit, and kept in position by electric locks. The armament was also charged and fired electrically. Tank believed that electrically-powered systems would be more reliable and more rugged than hydraulics; electric lines being much less prone to damage from enemy action.

The BMW 801 engine

Even before the first flight of the Fw 190 V1, BMW was bench testing a larger, more powerful 14-cylinder two-row radial engine, the BMW 801. This engine introduced an engine management system called *kommandogerät* ('brain box') – in effect, a mechanical computer which set mixture, propeller pitch (for the constant speed propeller), boost, and magneto timing. This reduced the pilot's workload

Design, development & prototypes

to the throttle control although there was a drawback inasmuch that minor surges made the Fw 190 harder to fly in close formation.

The RLM convinced Focke-Wulf and BMW to abandon the BMW 139 in favour of the new engine. While the 14-cylinder BMW 801 engine was similar in diameter to the 139 it was heavier and longer by a considerable margin. This required Tank to redesign the Fw 190, as a result of which the **V3** and **V4** were abandoned and the **V5** became the first prototype with the new engine, being fitted with a 1,539hp BMW 801C-0. Much of the airframe was strengthened and the cockpit was moved further back along the fuselage, which reduced the vexing problem of high temperatures and for the first time provided space for a nose armament. The 12-blade cooling fan became standardised for all subsequent BMW-powered Fw 190s and the oil cooler was protected by an armoured ring which made up the front face of the cowling. A small hole in the centre of the spinner also directed airflow to ancillary components.

On the V5, which first flew in the early spring of 1940, the sliding canopy was redesigned by replacing the rear Plexiglas glazing with duralumin panels. The fin shape was also changed and the rudder tab was replaced by a metal trim strip adjustable only on the ground. New, stiffer undercarriage struts were introduced, along with larger diameter mainwheels and new fairings of a simplified design were fitted to the legs.

At first, the V5 used the same wing as the first two prototypes, but to accommodate the larger diameter mainwheels, the wheel wells were enlarged

This page:
Port and starboard views of the Fw 190A's cockpit showing the control column with gun selector switch on the top; rudder pedals with heel guards and foot straps; left-hand side console throttle lever; main instrument dial board with altimeter, airspeed indicator, artificial horizon, compass, fuel gauge and rate of climb/descent indicator dials; and starboard side circular canopy actuator drive.

by moving forward part of the leading edge of the wing root. In this form this prototype was called the **V5k** for *kleine fläche* (small wing). Nevertheless, the weight increase was substantial, 635kg (1,400lb), resulting in higher wing loading and a deterioration in handling. As a result, following a collision with a ground vehicle in August 1940 that sent the V5 back to the factory for major repairs, it was rebuilt with a new wing which was less tapered in plan than the original design and had a larger area with a 10.506m (34ft 5in) span. The aircraft was now dubbed the **V5g** for *grosse fläche* (large wing). Although it was 10km/h (6.2mph) slower than when fitted with the small wing, V5g was much more manoeuvrable and had a faster climb rate. This new wing platform was to be used for all major production versions of the Fw 190A series.

Even with the new engine and cooling fan, the BMW 801 suffered from exceptionally high rear-row cylinder head temperatures, which, in at least one case is thought to have resulted in the premature detonation of the ammunition provided for the newly introduced cowling-mounted MG 17s. One other shortcoming of the cockpit location was a poor over-the-nose view which led to handling problems on the ground.

Fw 190A-0

The Fw 190A-0 was the pre-production series ordered in November 1940. Twenty-eight of these were built and because they were built before the new wing design had been fully tested and approved, the first nine Fw 190A-0s had small wings. All were armed with two synchronised 7.92mm MG 17 machine guns mounted in the engine cowling, one MG 17 in each wing root, and one MG 17 mid-span in each wing for a total of six rifle-calibre weapons. In detail, they were different from later A-series in that they had shorter spinners, the armoured cowling ring was a different shape with a scalloped hinge on the upper forward edge, and the bulges covering the interior air intakes on the engine cowlings were symmetrical 'teardrops'. Also, the panels aft of the exhaust pipes had no cooling slots. Several of these aircraft were later modified to test engines and specialised equipment.

Engine problems plagued the Fw 190 for much of its early development, and the entire project was threatened several times following a number of RLM commissions that recommended the programme be terminated. Had it not been for the input of *Oberleutnant*s Karl Borris and Otto Behrens, both of whom had originally enlisted in the Luftwaffe as mechanics, the Fw 190 programme might well have died before reaching operational status. Borris and Behrens could see beyond the initial teething problems and appreciated the formidable nature of the fighter and what it might be capable of given the opportunity to prove itself. Both men vigorously promoted the type's outstanding qualities which more than outweighed any perceived deficiencies.

Below: Frontal view of a Fw 190A-0 or A-1, showing the original wing root-mounted 7.92mm MG 17s and outboard wing-mounted 20mm MG-FF cannon.

Into service

The first unit to be equipped with the Fw 190A-0 was *Erprobungsstaffel 190*, an experimental unit manned by II/JG 26 '*Schlageter*' personnel, formed in March 1941 to help iron out the technical difficulties and approve the new fighter before it would be accepted for full operations in mainstream Luftwaffe service. At first this unit, commanded by *Oberleutnant* (*Oblt*) Behrens, was based at Rechlin, but it was soon moved to Le Bourget, Paris. Some fifty modifications were required before the RLM finally approved the Fw 190 for deployment to Luftwaffe units.

Fw 190A-1 and A-2

The first production Fw 190A-1s rolled off the assembly lines in June 1941 with the first few going to *Erprobungsstaffel 190* at Rechlin to join the pre-production Fw 190A-0s there for further testing. Following the delivery of these 'test' airframes, the Fw 190 A-1 entered operational service in July with 6./JG 26 being the first *Staffel*, followed by the rest of *II Gruppe*, in August 1941, which had by this time temporarily moved to Le Bourget to work up on the new type before returning to its original base at Moorseele in Belgium.

The Fw 190A-1 was powered by a 1,540hp BMW 801C-1 engine. However, the ongoing overheating problems experienced by the prototype Fw 190s during testing continued to affect the aircraft resulting in their engines having to be replaced after only 30 to 40 hours of use, sometimes less, with engine ground fires being a frequent hazard. Very heavy exhaust staining down the sides of the forward fuselage was also a feature of these early machines.

Armament comprised two 7.92mm MG 17s in the engine cowling, two wing root-mounted MG 17s (with all four synchronized to fire through the propeller arc) and two outboard wing-mounted 20mm (.78in) MG-FF/M cannon. A new, slightly longer, propeller spinner was fitted while the cowling sides featured reshaped asymmetric 'teardrop' bulges that directed the air flow around the engine cylinders; which remained the same shape for the rest of the A to G series. The panel immediately behind the exhaust outlets was plain i.e., unslotted, although some A-1s were later retrofitted with A-2/A-3 style cooling slots.

Above:
By the beginning of 1943, III./JG 1's Stab flight had received examples of the Fw 190A-2, and this photograph shows werknummer 0485 flown by the Gruppen Adjutant, Leutnant Deterra, in early 1943. Of interest is the marked tonal contrast between the upper surface colours and lack of mottling on the fuselage sides. III./JG 1's stylised Maltese Cross on a white shield with a red border is carried under the windscreen.

Above:
An early Fw 190A-1, probably from 5./JG 26 judging by the black horizontal Gruppe bar outlined in white – one of the first units to be equipped with the new type in August 1941 (following 6./JG 26 which received its first examples in July). Note the heavy exhaust staining on the forward fuselage and the diffused mottling on the rear fuselage sides, fin and rudder.

The new fighter was soon in action and claimed its first 'kill' on 14 August, when 6 *Staffel*'s *Staffelkapitän*, *Oblt* Walter Schneider, claimed a Spitfire shot down over Dunkirk. The type's first operational loss occurred a month later, on 18 September, when II JG 26's *Gruppenkommandeur*, *Hauptman* Walter Adolph was shot down and killed.

Focke-Wulf AG (AG = Corporation) completed 102 Fw 190A-1s at the Bremen and Marienburg factories between June and late October 1941 and these were followed by the Fw 190A-2 powered by the BMW 801C-2. First introduced that October, the A-2 marked a definite shift in air supremacy over the RAF whose main frontline fighter was the Spitfire Vb. The A-2's wing armament was increased by replacing the two wing root machine guns with two 20mm MG 151/20E cannon, the introduction of which led to the replacement of the Revi C12/C gunsight by the C12/D model.

Into service

This page and opposite page bottom: Three views of Fw 190A-2, 'Black 3' of 5./JG 1, based at Katwijk, Netherlands, in the summer of 1942 and flown by Oberfähnrich Ernst Terborg. The Gruppe's famous 'Tatzelwurm', a mythical worm-like serpent from Nordic folklore, was applied on the cowling sides in red i.e., 5 Staffel's colour. Note the high sheen on 'Black 3's paintwork and the 'spotty' mottling on the fuselage sides. The cowling underside may have been painted yellow while the spinner tip is thought to have been red.

Above:
Focke-Wulf Fw 190A-2, werknummer 332, possibly 'White 1' of I./JG 5, based at Herdla, Norway, late 1942. The Gruppe was known for applying exceptionally large staffel numerals to its aircraft, and those on this aircraft, and '6' in the background, are thought to have been white, for 1 Staffel, (or possibly yellow with a thin white outline for 3 Staffel.) Again, note the relatively high contrast between the upper surface colours on the wings and tailplanes, (which might indicate the use of the RLM 71 Dunkelgrün/RLM Grau 02 scheme?), which matches one of the very early patterns applied to Fw 190s.

Engine reliability problems, particularly overheating, continued well into the spring of 1942, together with the poor availability of the A-2's BMW 801C-2 engine. A related problem was the lower cylinder of the rear bank, which suffered broken connecting rods due to overheating. The problem was resolved by re-routing part of the exhaust system, a method discovered by III./JG 26's Technical Officer (TO) Rolf Schrödeter. To quickly implement the fix, it was found the re-routing could be done easily in airfield workshops and the subsequent reduction in temperature affecting the bottom cylinder went a long way to solving the overheating problem.

When the first of the A-2s appeared in October 1941, a further order for 315 A-1s subcontracted to AGO (Apparatebau GmbH Oschersleben) were built as A-2s. Powered by the BMW 801C-2, each had the re-routed exhaust manifold modification implemented on the production line, which, together with the addition of vertical ventilation slots on either side of the forward fuselage further aided cooling and finally resolved most of the type's overheating difficulties.

There were thirteen exhaust manifolds for the fourteen cylinders: eight were grouped to exit along the forward fuselage (four on each side just above the leading edge of the wing) and five under the forward centre section, between the undercarriage bays, with cylinders 9 and 10 sharing a common manifold.

Fw 190A-3

German production records make no real distinction between the Fw 190A-2 and the next sub-type, the Fw 190A-3, which was very similar – the total combined A-2 and A-3 production being approximately 910 airframes built between October 1941 and August 1942. In addition to Focke-Wulf and AGO, a new sub-contractor, Arado, at Warnemünde, also built A-2s and A-3s.

The Fw 190A-3 entered service in the spring of 1942. Powered by a 1,677hp BMW 801D-2 engine with an improved supercharger and a raised compression ratio which assisted take-off performance, the 801D-2 became the Fw 190's first really reliable engine, one that largely eliminated the problems that had dogged the type. Because of these changes, however, A-3's now required 100 octane fuel (C3) as opposed to the 87 Octane (B4) used by the A-2.

The A-3 retained the four-cannon wing of its predecessors as a production standard and featured minor cowling modifications. Following initial production, the A-3's FuG 7 HF radio was switched to the FuG 16 VHF radio, with more power and longer range. The type also introduced the *Umrüstbausätz* factory conversion sets, the Fw 190A-3/U3 being technically the first of the *Jagdbombers* (*Jabo* – fighter bombers) with an ETC 501 centreline bomb rack, mounted in a long streamlined ventral fairing and capable of carrying up to 500kg (1,100lb) of bombs or a 300-litre (66-gallon) drop tank. Some A-2s were also retrofitted with the ETC 501 racks, both sub-types being able to carry a 250kg (551lb) or 500kg bomb or four 50kg (110lb) bombs on an ER 4 adaptor. These *Jabo*s retained the cowl-mounted 7.92mm MG 17s and the wing root-mounted 20mm MG 151 cannon, but invariably deleted the outer MG-FF cannon.

A reconnaissance version of the Fw 190A-3 designated **A-3/U4** was equipped with two RB 12.5 cameras in the rear fuselage and a EK 16 gun camera in the leading edge of the port wing root. Armament was similar to the /U3 variant and the ETC 501 rack was often fitted with a 300-litre drop tank.

Many of the early Fw 190A-2s and A-3s had relatively long lives. The fluid nature of the Luftwaffe's air war saw aircraft transferring from units and theatres of operations often via maintenance and repair facilities. Older variants were typically passed on to training units or even re-engined to re-equip other fighter units. In fact, JG 5 was one unit that was still flying A-2 and A-3 variants towards the end of the war.

With the exception of JG 2 and 26, most of the Luftwaffe's fighter units that had been operating in France, were transferred to bases in the east following the launch of Operation *Barbarossa* in June 1941, but it wasn't until late August 1942 that I *Gruppe* JG 51 became the first fighter unit to re-equip with the Fw 190 on the Eastern Front. Introduced to the theatre when the German armies in the east had been all but checked, the Fw 190's wide track undercarriage came into its own on the basic Russian landing strips and of course the type allowed the carriage of bombs on the under fuselage ETC 501 carrier pending the introduction of dedicated fighter-bomber variants.

The first Fw 190 *Jabo*s
By early July 1942, 10./JG 2 and 10./JG 26 had converted from the Bf 109F-4/B to Fw 190A-2s and A-3s, fitted with the fuselage centreline ETC 501 rack. As mentioned previously, when the bomb rack was fitted it was normal to remove the outer pair of wing MG-FF 20mm cannon, but when this *Jabo* sub-type was superseded in September 1942 by the Fw 190A-4/U3 four MG 151 wing cannon were generally fitted.

JG 2's and JG 26's dedicated *Jabo Staffeln* maintained pressure on southern England. During the first months of their existence 10.(*Jabo*)/JG 2 and 10.(*Jabo*)/JG 26, initially flying Bf 109F-4/Bs, enjoyed considerable success against shipping and port installations around the south coast, and towards the end of June 1942, the two *Jabo Staffeln* were re-equipped with the bomb-carrying Fw **190A-2/U3** and **A-3/U3**.

Despite the famous *Staffelkapitän* of 10./JG 2. *Hptm* Frank Liesendahl being shot down in his Fw 190A-2 'Blue 14' W.Nr 439 on 14 July 1942 while attacking

Below:
Fw 190A-2, W/Nr 20282, 'Yellow 2' of 9./JG 2, based at Théville, France, June 1942. This particular aircraft was flown by Uffz Ludwig Hartmann and was finished in the standard RLM 74/75/76 'greys' scheme, but with the camouflage on the fuselage as a densely diffused application halfway down the sides of RLM 02 rather than a distinct mottle. The cowling underside and rudder were painted in RLM 04 Gelb, with the 'last three' of the werknummer '282' on the fin tip and ten 'kill' markings on the rudder.

Above:
Fw 190A-2, (possibly W/Nr 20252), 'Yellow 7' of 9./JG 2 with more conventional, but densely applied, mottling on the fuselage sides. Again, the rudder was painted yellow, with the last three digits of the werknummer (possibly 252) on the fin tip and a single 'kill' marking on the rudder.

shipping off Brixham; and 10./JG 26's *Staffelkapitän Oblt* Geburtig being lost over Littlehampton in his Fw 190A-3 'Black 1' W.Nr 7003 on 30 July 1942, *Jabo* missions continued unabated through the summer. These low-level surprise attacks mounted by the Fw 190 *Jabo*s were almost impossible to counter and were colloquially referred to as 'tip and run' raids by the British. One particular raid on Canterbury at the end of October 1942, consisting of over one hundred Fw 190s from JG 2 and JG26 *Jabo Staffeln*, escorted by the units' Fw 190 fighters, became the largest daylight raid on England since 1940.

In February 1943, 10.(*Jabo*)/JG 26 became 10.(*Jabo*)/JG 54, (although it still remained under the control of JG 26), but the success achieved by these two *Staffeln*, together never totalling more than about thirty or so aircraft at any one time, eventually prompted a fuller re-organisation of the *Jabo* concept.

Fw 190A-4

Introduced in July 1942 and replacing the A-3 on the production line, the Fw 190A-4 was equipped with the same BMW 801D-2 engine and armament as the A-3, while the fin top now included a re-designed aerial mount, a feature that was to be retained throughout all remaining Fw 190 production following the introduction of the FuG 16Z radio that now became standard. In some sub-variants, controllable engine cooling vents were fitted to the fuselage sides in place of the plain slots.

By the beginning of 1943, daytime raids over western Europe by US 8th Air Force bombers, increasingly escorted by long-range fighters, were becoming more frequent as the Americans took the first steps to achieving their goal of air superiority. From this time onwards the *Jagdwaffe*'s primary mission would become the defence of the Reich. The four *Gruppen* of JG 1, the day fighter unit defending Holland and northern Germany, was re-equipped with the Fw 190A-3 and A-4. Additional cover was provided by withdrawing *Gruppen* from other fronts as the Luftwaffe's training organisation was simply not geared up for a rapid expansion of *Jagdgeschwader* numbers. In April 1943, by using the simple expedient of splitting units into two, I and III./JG 1 formed the basis of a new *Jagdgeschwader*, JG 11.

Initial encounters with the USAAF bomber formations had revealed shortcomings in the high altitude performance of the BMW 801D-2. Consequently, one of the first performance-enhancing installations to be developed was the adaptation of the 801D-2 to accept a water-methanol mixture (MW 50) which raised power to 2100hp for a short period – literally minutes. Nevertheless, due to delays in MW 50 production, this system was not introduced on the Fw 190A-4. However, the Fw 190A-4's principal improvement was related to the number of weapon and equipment packages that could be fitted to enhance its capabilities beyond that of a pure interceptor alone. Such packages were trialled using factory-fitted *Umrüstbausätz* kits (as they were termed); in-the-field-designed *Rüstsätz* kits, or combinations of both.

The Fw 190A-4 series include the following:

Fw 190A-4/U1: a fighter-bomber modification with an under-fuselage mounted ETC 501 bomb rack and a reduced armament of two wing root mounted MG 151/20E cannon.

Fw 190A-4/U3: another fighter-bomber variant with the same armament as the /U1, but with an uprated BMW 801D-2 engine. Some Fw 190A-4/U3s were adapted for night operations and had a landing light mounted in the leading edge of the port wing root.

Fw 190A-4/U4: a reconnaissance fighter with two Rb 12.4 cameras in the rear fuselage and an EK 16 or Robot II gun camera. It retained both cowl-mounted MG 17s and a pair of MG 151 wing root cannon.

Fw 190A-4/U7: In a further attempt to improve high altitude performance, additional compressor air intakes were fitted on either side of the cowling in lieu of the teardrop fairings, but as the new installation affected the /U7's top speed the development wasn't widely adopted although Adolf Galland did fly it in the spring of 1943.

Fw 190A-4/U8: a long-range fighter-bomber with two 300-litre drop tanks on VTr Ju 87 racks, with duralumin fairings produced by Weserflug mounted under the wings and a centreline bomb rack. The outer wing-mounted 20mm MG-FF/M cannon and the cowling-mounted MG 17s were removed to save weight. The /U8 was operated by SKG 10 on its nocturnal raids over southern England, and effectively became the forerunner of a newer, extended range, fighter-bomber or '*Jabo-Rei*' (*Jagdbomber mit vergrosserter Reichweite*) under the designation Fw 190G.

Fw 190A-4/R6: Amongst the first widely used *Rüstsätz* kits tested on the Fw 190A-4, under the designation A-4/R6, (although it did not enter service in any

Below: Powered by the BMW 801C-2, the Fw 190A-2 had the exhaust manifold re-route modification implemented on the production line, which, together with the addition of vertical ventilation slots on the side of the forward fuselage further aided cooling and finally resolved most of the type's overheating problems. This particular Fw 190A-2, 'White 4' of 1./JG 26, seen at Tricqueville, Normandy, on the Channel Coast, has a very heavily mottled fuselage that contrasts sharply with the yellow rudder.

Above:
Fw 190A-2, W/Nr 20206 of Stab III./JG 26 photographed in between sorties in the summer 1942. Modellers might wish to note the angles of the control surfaces, with ailerons, flaps, elevators and rudder all slightly displaced. The playing card '7 of spades' with a name is presumably a personal badge.

Right:
Later deliveries of Fw 190A-1s and Fw 190A-2s were probably finished in the standard 'mid-war greys' of RLM 74 Dunkelgrau and RLM 75 Mittlegrau upper surfaces with RLM 76 Lichtblau under surfaces. This particular Fw 190A-2, possibly of JG 2, features an additional camouflage effect, seen on several early Fw 190s, a criss-cross pattern along the leading edges of the mainplanes. Note the yellow cowling underside and stylised black exhaust stain masking panel.

numbers until the introduction of the A-5), was the air-to-air missile launcher WGr 21 *'Werfer Granat'* or 'stove pipe', which fired time-fused explosive shells designed to break up American bomber 'box formations'. Aircraft so equipped were often referred to *'Pulk Zerstörern'*.

The first of the *Rüstsätz* field kits, introduced in 1943 and fitted to the A-4 was the A-4/R1, and comprised a FuG 16ZY radio set with a Morane 'whip' aerial under the port wing. These aircraft, called *Leitjäger* or Fighter Formation Leaders, could be tracked and directed from the ground via special radio equipment called *Y-Verfahren*. More frequent use of this apparatus was made following the introduction of the Fw 190 A-5 and subsequent versions.

The increasing obsolescence of the Ju 87 'Stuka' and the ability of the Fw 190 to carry bombs meant that the latter was ideal for development into a close support fighter to equip the Luftwaffe's tactical air support units which were undergoing reorganisation and re-designation as *Schlachtgeschwader*. The huge advantage that the Fw 190 enjoyed in the ground attack role was simply that it required no escort. Having released its bombs it reverted to being a fighter; consequently several *Schlachtgeschwader* pilots gained quite large numbers of aerial victories. As the Wehrmacht went on the defensive on the Russian Front in early 1943, pure fighter variants of the Fw 190 were in short supply, with only JG 54 operating the fighter in the air superiority role by the end of the year. The hard-pressed German Army required all available air assets to be used for ground attack purposes, and as the Ju 87 crews were finding it increasingly difficult to survive given the 'Stuka's' low speed and the formidable flak

and fighter defences now encountered, its production was discontinued and replaced by ground attack variants of the Fw 190.

The Fw 190A-4's maximum speed was 670kph (416mph) at 6,250m (20,590ft). Operational ceiling was 11,400m (37,400ft). Normal range was around 800km (497 miles). Approximately 976 Fw 190A-4s were built between June 1942 and March 1943.

Fw 190A-5

The Fw 190A-5 was developed after it was determined that the Fw 190 could easily carry more ordnance. Focke-Wulf's design team became convinced that planned additional armament would move the aircraft's centre of gravity. The best solution to counter this was to move the BMW 801D-2 engine forward by adding a 150mm (5.9in) engine mount extension which was introduced on all production lines. In place of the ventilation slots, engine cowling shutters controlled from the cockpit were installed and the rear fuselage equipment compartment cover was enlarged. Standard armament did not change and remained at two cowl-mounted

This page:
Two views of Fw 190A-3, W/Nr 2187, 'Black 11' of 8./JG 2, based at Brest, France summer 1942. During the summer of 1942, the black painted exhaust-masking area, which was applied to many early JG 2 Fw 190s, was 'developed' with an eagle's head being painted forward of it on the cowling sides. Often this was only applied to the port side, with III Gruppe's cockerel's head on the starboard side. Another 'innovation' introduced by JG 2 around this time, was the painting-out of the black centre to the fuselage balkenkreuze with camouflage colours, as illustrated on 'Black 11'. Camouflage was the standard RLM 74/75/76 scheme, with a fairly high, fuselage demarcation line with diffused mottling. The cowling underside and rudder were in RLM 04 Gelb and the 'last four' of the werknummer was painted on the fin tip. The small size of the III Gruppe vertical bar is noteworthy.

Above and below:
Fw 190A-3, W/Nr 135313, of Stab III./JG 2, which accidentally landed at RAF Pembrey on 23 June 1942 following a dogfight with RAF Spitfires. The pilot, Oberleutnant Armin Faber, III./JG 2's Adjutant became disorientated during the combat and mistook the Bristol Channel for the English Channel and flew north instead of south, thinking South Wales was France, and turned towards the nearest airfield – RAF Pembrey. He was immediately captured, along with his aircraft (the first Fw 190 to fall into British hands intact) and spent the rest of the war as a PoW. At this time Pembrey was host to No.1 Air Gunners School which flew Bristol Blenheim Is and IVs, several of which may be seen in the background.

MG 17s with two MG 151/20E and two MG-FF cannon in the wings. Solid, forged mainwheel hubs replaced the earlier mainwheel hub with its six circular openings from the A-5 onwards.

Some A-5s were fitted with the MW 50 installation using a mix of 50 per

Above:
Fw 190A-2, 'White 11' of 7./JG 2, based at Théville, France, summer 1942. Individual staffeln started to apply unit badges during the summer of 1942, and this example from 7 Staffel, JG 2 features the unit's famous 'thumb squashing a top hat' marking on the cowling, first introduced on the unit's Bf 109Es during the summer of 1940. Finished in the RLM 74/75/76 'greys' scheme, diffused areas of mottling were carried on the fuselage sides and fin. The cowling underside and rudder appear to have been painted the lighter yellow RLM 27 Gelb shade although this may just be a trick of the light or the type of film used. The werknummer doesn't appear to have been applied to the fin tip. Of note is the excessive exhaust staining, which was often disguised by an area of black paint, usually thinly outlined in white with black trim, which was starting to be introduced on the Fw 190s around this period.

cent methanol alcohol and 50 per cent water which could be injected into the engine to produce a short-term power boost, but the system was not adopted for mass production. New radio gear, including FuG 25a Erstling IFF, and an electric artificial horizon also found their way into the A-5 which retained the same basic armament fit as the A-4. A small batch of Fw 190A-5s were fitted with external turbo supercharger inlets on the engine cowling sides, but they were not widely used because of the aerodynamic drag they created.

Over the Reich, the USAAF's four-engine bombers were proving extremely tough opponents, with each bomber requiring numerous hits from 20mm cannon to bring it down; consequently, it was usual for two or more fighters to attack a single bomber together. Some success was met with head-on attacks against the bombers' poorly armoured and defended nose and cockpit areas, thus all *Verbandsführer* (formation leaders) were urged to ensure that *Rotten*, *Schwärm*, and even *Gruppen* wherever possible, were assembled to attack from the front in order to concentrate their combined firepower against the bombers' most vulnerable section of airframe. In so doing of course, frontal attacks caused closing speeds to increase rapidly, vastly reducing the available firing-time for both fighter pilot and

Above:
Fw 190A-2/U3, W/Nr 122080, 'Blue 6' of 10./(Jabo)/JG 2 being serviced at Caen-Carpiquet, France August 1942. The centreline ETC 501 bomb rack has been removed and the port fuselage side radio hatch is open. The /U3 retained the wing root-mounted 20mm MG 151 cannon and fuselage-mounted 7.92mm MG 17s, with the outer MG-FF being removed. 'Blue 6', a modified A-2 upgraded to A-3 standard, was camouflaged in the RLM 74/75/76 scheme, with large areas of diffused mottling on the fuselage and fin. As with the Western Front dedicated fighter units, the Jabo's cowling underside and rudder were painted in yellow. Although not visible in this view, the Staffel's fox with a broken ship in its jaws badge would have been carried on the cowling sides. The chevron and horizontal bar 'Jabo' marking adopted by 10(Jabo)./JG 2 is clearly visible on the rear fuselage.

defending gunner alike when compared to the relatively 'slow' closing speed of a stern attack.

In order for individual wingmen to identify their particular *Verbandsführer*, special markings were developed to facilitate easy and rapid identification. The Fw 190A-5s of JG 1 for instance were painted with white or yellow engine cowlings, or black and white checks or broad horizontal stripes. *Schwärmführer* carried red diagonal stripes along the fuselage sides appearing as a Vee from above and *Staffelkapitän* often had their aircraft's fin/rudder's painted white.

Certain Focke-Wulf 190A-5 were fitted with the *Umrüstbausätz* /U12, that was specially created for attacking bombers. Fitted with MG 151s inboard, the MG-FF cannon were replaced with two external underwing packs each containing two 20mm MG 151 cannon. As the gun packs were underslung, warm air from the engine was ducted into them via the wing leading edge to prevent the weapons from freezing. The **A-5/U12** became the prototype installation of what was known as the R1 package from the A-6 onwards.

The Fw 190A-5 also saw several other *Umrüstbausätz* kits fitted. The **A-5/U2** was designed as a night *Jabo-Rei* and featured exhaust flame dampers. A centreline ETC 501 rack typically held a 250kg bomb, and wing mounted racks carried 300-litre drop tanks. An EK 16 gun camera, as well as landing lights, were fitted to the wing leading edge. The /U2 was armed with only two 20mm MG 151 cannon. The **A-5/U3** was another *Jabo* fighter, fitted with an ETC 501 rack for drop tanks or bombs and it too featured only two MG 151s for armament. The **A-5/U4** was a reconnaissance fighter with two RB 12.5 cameras and the armament of the basic A-5 with the exception of the MG-FF cannon.

In June 1943, a detachment of WGr 21-equipped Fw 190A-5s from the *Erprobungskommando 25*, (a test unit set up in 1943 at Achmer to develop anti-bomber weapons) was attached to I./JG 1 and became the first operational unit to test this new device. JG 1 also tested an experimental twin-tube *Doppelrohren Werfer* installation. During May 1944, 12./JG 3 tested a rearward firing rocket launcher slung under the fuselage called *Krebsgerät* WGr 21 which was used operationally by the so-called *Dödelstaffel* of II./JG 300 although the fitment never received a *Rüstsätz* number.

By June 1944 and the invasion of Normandy, even 'pure' fighter *Gruppen* from JG 26 were flying WGr 21 missions against Allied bombers. The rocket tubes could be removed quickly to allow fighter missions to be flown as the installation had a detrimental effect on the fighter's performance, in particular raising the Fw 190's stalling speed by some 30kph (18.6mph), which meant that the aircraft had to be flown onto the ground when landing.

The **A-5/U8** was another *Jabo-Rei*. Equipped with two MG 151 cannon it also carried centreline-mounted SC 250 (250kg /551lb) bombs and underwing 300-litre drop tanks. This sub-type later became the Fw 190G-2.

Above:
Fw 190A-3, W/Nr 2134, 'Black 1', of 5./JG 1, flown by the Staffelkapitän, Oblt Max Bucholz, based at Woensdrecht, Netherlands, summer 1942. The white rings on the spinner are thought to be staffelkapitän identification markings, and 5 Staffel's red 'Tatzelwurm' was carried on the cowling side. 'Black 1', was finished in the standard 'mid-war greys' scheme and had quite defined mottling along the fuselage and fin sides. Only the cowling underside was yellow (not the rudder). The white 'marking' under the cockpit is the wing of a stylised eagle silhouette. Oblt Max Bucholz claimed 28 victories before transferring to staff duties in 1943.

Below:
An intriguing photo of an otherwise anonymous early Fw 190A sub-type. The lack of a barrel protruding from the wing root would indicate the fitting of an MG 17 machine gun (as per the A-1), although engine exhaust slots are present suggesting the aircraft is a later A-2 or A-3 without wing root armament. Of additional interest is the very dense fuselage mottle which was fairly common amongst early versions of the A-series. The cowling underside is yellow (RLM Gelb 04) as is the rudder. The Dornier Do 217E-4 in the background with white wing and fuselage bands dates the photo to around November/December 1942 and Fall Anton (Operation Anton), the occupation of Vichy France.

Above:
Fw 190A-3s undergoing final assembly, possibly at Focke-Wulf's factory at Marienburg in Germany, which produced approximately half of all Fw 190s produced. In this image the 190's inner mainwheel doors are readily apparent, however, they were often removed in operational service and not fitted at all on later sub-types.

This page:
Two views of Fw 190A-2, W/Nr 312, with a collapsed port undercarriage leg presumably before allocation to a front line unit as it still wears its factory codes (stammkennzeichen) CM+CK on the fuselage sides and under the wings. The cowling underside appears to be yellow further indicating delivery to a base along the Channel coastline, as indeed the name on the factory wall behind (J. De La Porte) might indicate. However, according to the captions accompanying these photos, the aircraft was photographed at an unidentified location in Denmark after the German surrender in May 1945. The gouges in the grass would indicate that the aircraft was moving sideways when the undercarriage leg collapsed although only one propeller blade appears to be damaged. (Both images via NMD)

Opposite page top:
The reconnaissance version of the Fw 190A-3 was designated A-3/U4 and was equipped with two RB 12.5 cameras in the rear fuselage (just visible behind the cockpit entry step). Issued to one of the Fernaufklärungsgruppen, for long range (strategic) reconnaissance duties, 'Black 10' was finished in the standard 'mid war greys' RLM 74 Dunkelgrau and RLM 75 Mittlegrau upper surfaces with RLM 76 Lichtblau under surfaces and fuselage sides with dense but diffused mottling. The cowling underside and rudder appear to be yellow to comply with the tactical identification markings applied to single-engined fighters based along the Channel coastline.

Opposite page bottom:
Epitomising not only the fate of so many Fw 190s at the end of hostilities, but again the relative longevity of some of the earlier sub-types, this Fw 190A-3, W///Nr 2168, somehow survived until 1945, when it was found at Bad Aibling. It had obviously been progressively repainted since its production in early 1942, and was sporting late-war simplified national markings, but it's anybody's guess as to what the camouflage scheme was – a lesson in how difficult it is to determine colours from b&w photos.

Focke-Wulf Fw 190V1, werknummer 0001, D-OPEZ, the first prototype, Focke-Wulf works, Bremen, Germany, May 1939

D-OPEZ was originally finished in an overall natural metal scheme when it was first rolled out of the Focke-Wulf works at Bremen in May 1939. At this time no national markings were carried other than a black swastika (*hakenkreuz*) on a white circle surrounded by a red horizontal band across the fin and rudder – which was standard for civil aircraft – plus the civil registration D-OPEZ, on either side of the fuselage and spread out under the mainplanes – 'D-O' under the starboard wing and 'PEZ' under the port wing, reading from the rear. Note the large ducted spinner arrangement.

Focke-Wulf Fw 190V1, werknummer 0001, D-OPEZ, the first prototype, at the time of its first flight from the Focke-Wulf works airfield at Bremen, on 1 June 1939

Port and starboard profile views of D-OPEZ at the time of its first flight on 1 June 1939, flown by *Flugkapitän* Hans Sander. By this time, werknummer 0001 had been re-finished in the then standard Luftwaffe 'fighter aircraft' colours of RLM 70 *Schwarzgrün* and RLM 71 *Dunkelgrün* upper surfaces, in a sharp-edged 'splinter' pattern, with RLM 65 *Hellblau* under surfaces. Again, no national markings were carried other than a black swastika on a white circle surrounded by a red horizontal band across the fin and rudder and retention of the civil registration D-OPEZ, on either side of the fuselage and under the mainplanes. The large ducted spinner arrangement was retained.

Colour Profiles

Focke-Wulf Fw 190V1, werknummer 0001, FO+LY, after having a conventional engine cowling and spinner fitted in early 1940

The first prototype as it looked in early 1940, still finished in the Luftwaffe fighter 'splinter' scheme of RLM 70 *Schwarzgrün* and RLM 71 *Dunkelgrün* upper surfaces with RLM 65 *Hellblau* under surfaces, although the pattern looks to be slightly different to the one it wore in June 1939. Also, by this time the airframe had been transferred on to the military register and had standard Luftwaffe national markings applied – narrow-bordered crosses (*balkenkreuze*) above and below the wings and on the fuselage sides and a white outlined black swastika on the fin. The *stammkennzeichen* (factory code) FO+LY was applied to the fuselage sides, two letters either side of the fuselage cross, and under the mainplanes, two letters either side of the underwing crosses. The original large ducted spinner arrangement was replaced by a smaller, more conventional spinner that only covered the hub of the three-blade VDM propeller.

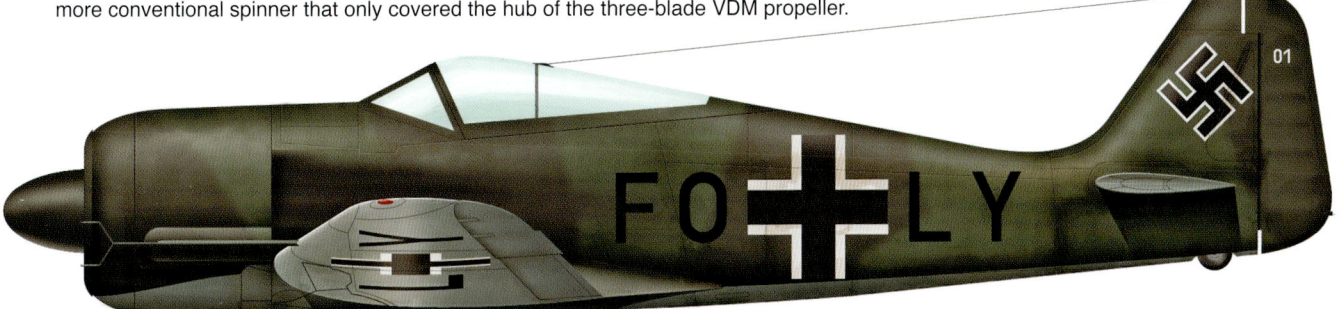

Focke-Wulf Fw 190A-0, werknummer 0027, '27', under test at the *Erprobungsstelle der Luftwaffe*, Rechlin, Germany, 1940

werknummer 0027, illustrated as it looked while undergoing testing at the *Erprobungsstelle der Luftwaffe* (Test Centre of the Air Force), Rechlin, Germany in 1940. The aircraft appears to be in an overall RLM 02 *Grau* scheme with red oxide primer on the fabric covered rudder. Narrow-bordered crosses (*balkenkreuze*) were carried above the wings with broader bordered crosses on the fuselage sides and under the mainplanes which had become standard by this time. A black swastika was carried on the fin, which was outlined in white thinly outlined in black. No *stammkennzeichen* (factory code) was applied at this stage, but the 'last two' of the werknummer, '27', was applied in white under the cockpit windscreen and on the cowling side. It has also been suggested (albeit unconfirmed) that the spinner might have been finished in RLM 23 *Rot* (red).

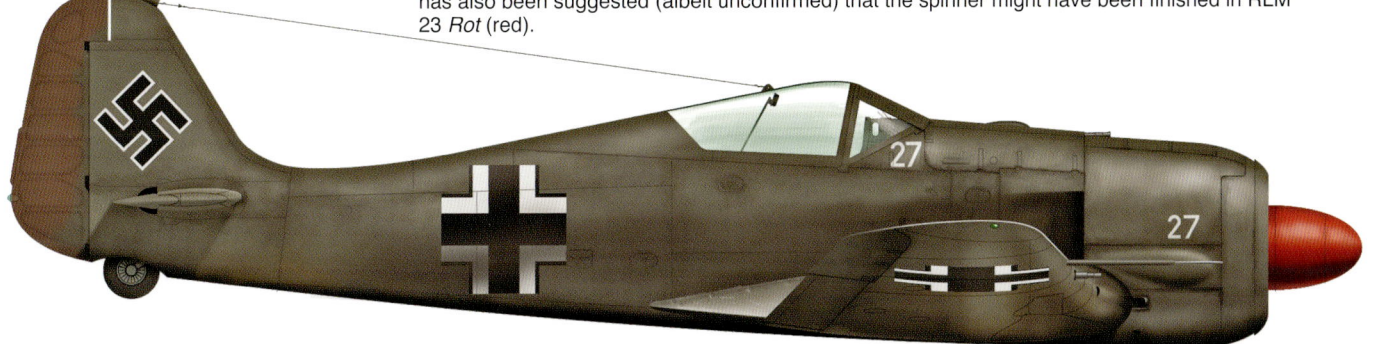

Focke-Wulf Fw 190A-0, werknummer 0020, KB+PV, based at the *Erprobungsstelle der Luftwaffe*, Rechlin, Germany, early 1941

werknummer 0020, was one of a small batch of pre-production Fw 190A-0s, which took part in service evaluation trials. Fitted with the now production standard wing and 20mm MG FF cannon in the outer wing positions, when these first Fw 190As came off the production line, contemporary photographs would suggest that they were finished in the then relatively new day-fighter scheme of RLM 74 *Dunkelgrau* and RLM 75 *Mittelgrau* upper surfaces in a soft-edged 'splinter' pattern with RLM 76 *Lichtblau* fuselage sides, fin and rudder and under surfaces. The fuselage mottle varied considerably in style and intensity on these early Fw 190As, KB+PV featuring a high fuselage demarcation line with subdued and restrained mottling applied to the fuselage sides, fin and rudder. Mottle colours are in RLM 70, 74 and 02. Standard narrow-bordered black and white crosses (*balkenkreuze*) were carried above the wings with broader bordered crosses on the fuselage sides and under the mainplanes, with a black swastika (*hakenkreuz*) on the fin, outlined in white and thinly bordered in black. The factory code KB+PV was applied in black to the fuselage sides either side of the fuselage cross and under the wings again, either side of the crosses – ie K+B, P+V. Note the spinner painted half white and half RLM 70 *Schwarzgrün*.

Focke-Wulf Fw 190A-2, werknummer 325, 'Yellow 13' of 3./JG 2, based at Tricqueville, France, summer 1942, flown by *Oberfeldwebel* Josef Heinzeller

By the time deliveries of the Fw 190A-2 were starting to reach the staffeln on the Channel Coast, the RLM 74/75/76 'mid-war greys' day-fighter scheme had become standardised, albeit initially with little or no mottling on the fuselage sides, fin and rudder. During the summer/early autumn of 1942, yellow rudders and cowling undersides were being seen increasingly on Fw 190s as tactical recognition markings and an aid to rapid identification of this still new type, generally in RLM 04 *Gelb*, (as illustrated here), or occasionally the paler RLM 27 *Gelb*. As well as staffel, Gruppe or Geschwader unit badges, individual personal markings were also occasionally applied to the cowling sides. This particular 3 Staffel machine featured a white profile of a 'Scottie' dog and the name 'Schnauzl' (apparently Ofw Heinzeller's pet dog), which had first been seen on his Bf 109E during the Battle of Britain. Note the 'last three' of the werknummer on the fin tip. The propeller spinner and propeller blades were both RLM 70 *Schwarzgrün*, the standard factory finish for these items.

Focke-Wulf Fw 190A-2, 'Black G and horizontal bars' of JG 26's Geschwaderstab, based at Brest-Guipavas, France, spring 1942, flown by *Hauptmann* Wilhelm Gäth

JG 26's Staffeln started to receive their first Fw 190A-2s in November 1941, and by the spring of 1942 the unit's Geschwaderstab had also received examples of the sub-type. Finished in the standard 'mid-war greys' scheme of RLM 74 *Dunkelgrau*/RLM 75 *Mittelgrau* upper surfaces, to the standard Fw 190 soft-edged 'splinter' pattern, with RLM 76 *Lichtblau* under surfaces and fuselage sides. The amount of fuselage side mottling still varied from very sparse to very dense as illustrated here. Whereas JG 26's Gruppe Stabsschwarme, (Wing Staff Flights), applied the more usual 'stab' chevron marking, many of the Geschwaderstab (Group Staff Flight) machines adopted horizontal bars in front and to the rear of the fuselage balkenkreuze with what is thought to have been the first, (one or two), letters of the pilot's surname in front, such as Hptm Wilhelm Gäth's 'G' illustrated here. The cowling underside and rudder were painted in RLM 04 *Gelb*. The propeller spinner and propeller blades were RLM 70 *Schwarzgrün*.

Focke-Wulf Fw 190A-2, WNr 20202, 'Black He and horizontal bars' of JG 26's Geschwaderstab, based at Brest-Guipavas, France, spring 1942, flown by *Oberfeldwebel* Bruno Hegenauer

Another example of utilising the letters of a pilot's surname, *Oberfeldwebel* Hegebauer's first two letters of his surname (He) was painted in front of the 'pointed' bar. Note how the upper case 'H' is thinly outlined in white but the lower case 'e' isn't. 'Black He' was camouflaged in the RLM 74/75/76 scheme, with a slightly lower fuselage demarcation line and diffused mottling. The cowling underside and rudder were painted in RLM 04 *Gelb*. Hegenauer had been credited with five victories by the time he was killed in action in May 1943.

Focke-Wulf Fw 190A-2, (WNr thought to be 093), 'White 9' of 7./JG 2, based at Théville, France, summer 1942, flown by *Lt* Willi Stratmann

Individual staffeln were starting to apply unit badges during the summer of 1942, and this example from 7 Staffel, JG 2 features the unit's famous 'thumb squashing a top hat' marking on the cowling, first introduced on the unit's Bf 109Es during the summer of 1940. Finished in the standard RLM 74/75/76 'greys' scheme, diffused areas of mottling were carried on the fuselage sides and fin. Only the rudder was painted in yellow and the 'last three' of the werknummer has been applied to the fin tip. Note the black painted exhaust-masking area, thinly outlined in white with black trim, which was starting to be introduced on the Fw 190s around this time.

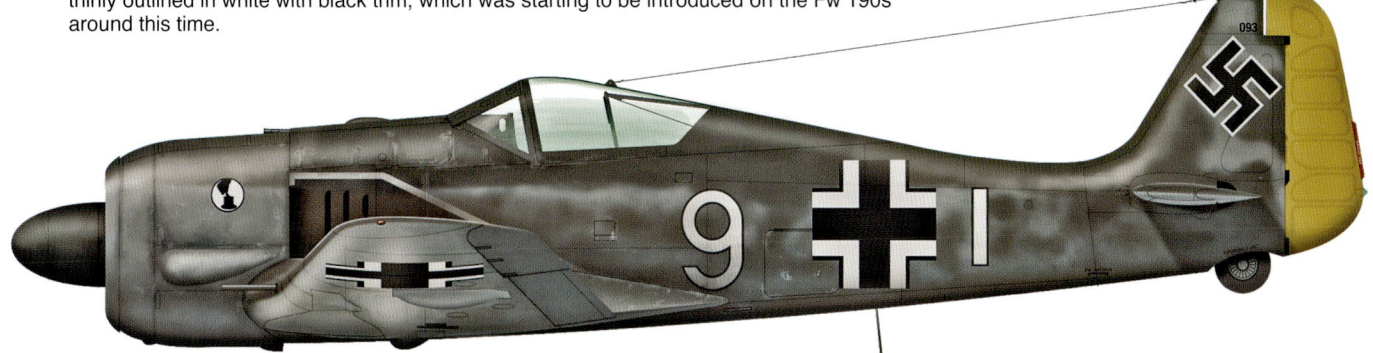

Focke-Wulf Fw 190A-3, WNr 0135403, 'White 10' of 7./JG 2, based at Théville, France, summer 1942

JG 2 were not long behind JG 26 in receiving examples of the then new A-3 sub-type, during the summer of 1942, which it operated alongside the earlier A-2s. Powered by a 1,677hp BMW 801D-2 engine with an improved supercharger, the A-3 required a higher 100 octane fuel (C3) but largely eliminated the problems that had plagued the A-1s and A-2s. Externally otherwise virtually identical to the A-2, it retained the same four wing cannon armament. 'White 7' was finished in the standard RLM 74/75/76 'mid-war greys' scheme. Just visible under the mottling along the fuselage sides is the painted-out factory code which is thought to be RC+TC. The cowling underside tray and the rudder were painted in RLM 04 *Gelb*, and the last three of the werknummer '403' was prefixed by the letters Wnr'.

Focke-Wulf Fw 190A-2, WNr 20235, 'Blue 4' of Einsatzstaffel/Jagdfliegerschule 2, based at Zerbst, Germany, 1942

Despite certain references attributing this particular airframe to Jagdfliegerschule 4, (the unit badges are very similar), it is more likely that it was operated by the Einsatzstaffel of Jagdfliegerschule 2, (a sub-unit of instructors and more experienced trainee pilots that could fly combat missions).

'Blue 4' is finished in the standard RLM 74/74/76 'mid-war greys' but note the low division of the upper and under surface colours along the fuselage. The blue (RLM 24 *Dunkelblau*?) numeral '4' is outlined in white and the tip of the propeller spinner is also RLM 24. JFS 2's unit badge, a red and blue shield, with a black winged arrow over a white triangle, was carried under the windscreen. The cowling underside was painted in RLM 04 *Gelb*. Jagdfliegerschule 2, which was formed in 1941 in Zerbst, was later disbanded and reformed as JG 102 in February 1943.

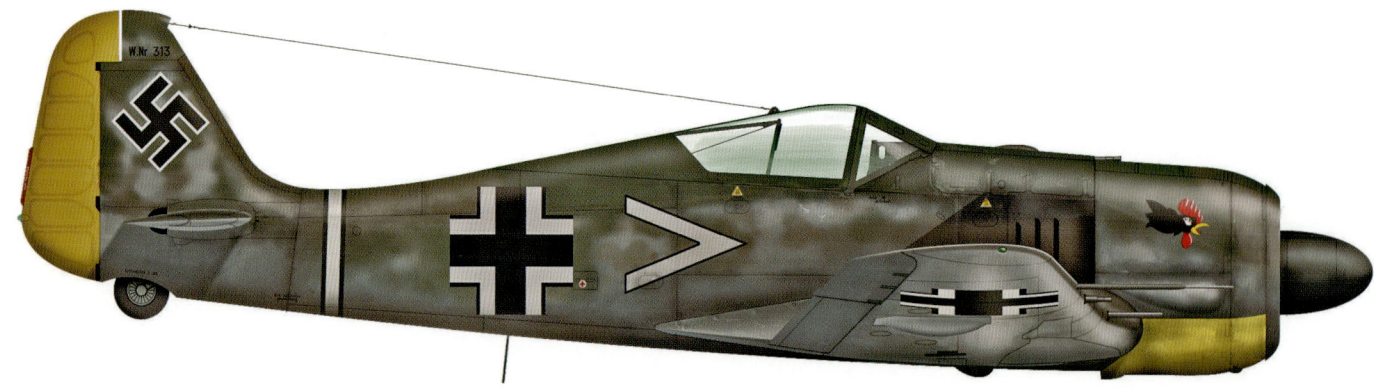

Focke-Wulf Fw 190A-3, WNr 135313, 'White chevron', of Stab III./JG 2, based at St Pol-Brias, France, June 1942, flown by *Oberleutnant* Armin Faber

Possibly one of the most recognisable Fw 190As. *Oberleutnant* Armin Faber was Adjutant of Stab III./JG 2, and on 23 June flew a combat mission with 7 Staffel, to intercept a force of RAF Bostons on their way back from a bombing mission. A dogfight developed over the English Channel with the escorting Spitfires, during which *Oblt* Faber became disorientated after shooting down a Spitfire of No 310 Squadron RAF. and mistook the Bristol Channel for the English Channel and flew north instead of south – thinking South Wales was France – and turned towards the nearest airfield, RAF Pembrey. Observers on the ground could not believe their eyes as Faber waggled his wings in a victory celebration, lowered the aircraft's undercarriage and landed. He was immediately captured, along with his aircraft and spent the rest of the war as a PoW.

Oblt Faber's A-3 was finished in the standard 'mid-war greys' scheme of RLM 74/RLM 75 upper surfaces, with RLM 76 *Lichtblau* under surfaces and fuselage sides. Mottling was very diffused and sparse. The cowling underside and rudder were RLM 04 *Gelb*, with the werknummer, prefixed by 'W.Nr.' on the port fin tip only. Note the unit's cockerel's head, adopted as the Gruppe badge from October 1941 (until early 1942), on both sides of the cowling and the way the III Gruppe bar completely encircles the rear fuselage. This aircraft was the first Fw 190 to fall into British hands intact and was subsequently repainted in RAF colours and evaluated by the Air Fighting Development Unit at Farnborough, providing the Allies with extremely valuable intelligence on the type.

Fw 190A-3, WNr 065, 'White 18' of 1./SG 101, Rheims, France, mid-1943

When the frontline Fw 190 units received improved examples of the type, the older sub-type survivors were invariably sent to Fliegerschulen (Flying Schools) to train the next generation of pilots. 'White 18' (WNr 065) is thought to be an A-3 and is illustrated in the markings of 1 Staffel, SG (Schlachtgeschwader – Ground Attack Wing) 101. SG 101 was formed in February 1943 at Reims, from Schlachtfliegerschule 1, to train pilots in ground attack methods using the Fw 190 and Henschel Hs 129. 'White 18' was finished in a well-worn and weathered standard RLM 74/75/76 'mid-war greys' scheme and still retains the Channel Front RLM 04 *Gelb* rudder and cowling undersides. The 'last three' of the werknummer '065' was repeated on the fin and the rudder. SG 101 was moved to Wischau, (now in the Czech Republic) in April 1944, and then to Aalborg-West in Denmark, where it was disbanded on 4th April 1945.

Focke-Wulf Fw 190A-3/U3, WNr 122080 'Blue 6', of 10(*Jabo*)./JG 2, based at Caen-Carpiquet, France, August 1942

10(*Jabo*)./JG 2 were initially equipped Bf 109F-4/Bs but towards the end of June 1942 started to re-equip with Fw 190A-2s and A-3s fitted with an ETC 501 centreline bomb rack, mounted in a long streamlined ventral fairing, which had the ability to carry a 250kg, 500kg, or four 50kg bombs on an ER 4 adaptor. 'Blue 6', a modified A-2 upgraded to A-3 standard, was camouflaged in the standard RLM 74/75/76 scheme, with a well-defined fuselage demarcation line with large areas of diffused mottling. As with the Channel Coast dedicated fighter units, the *Jabo*'s cowling underside and rudder were painted in yellow. The 'last three' of the werknummer '080' was applied to the fin tip. Note the staffel's fox badge with a ship in its jaws on the cowling, and the chevron and horizontal bar '*Jabo*' marking adopted by 10(*Jabo*)./JG 2 on the rear fuselage.

Focke-Wulf Fw 190A-3/U3, 'Black 6', of 14.(*Jabo*)/JG 5, based at Petsamo, Finland, summer 1943

JG 5's specialist fighter-bomber, '*Jabo*', unit, 14 Staffel, was formed at the beginning of 1943, on a mix of modified Fw 190A-2s and A-3s fitted with ETC 501 bomb racks. In keeping with other JG 5 staffeln, larger than standard numerals were applied, in black with a white outline, and most of the unit's aircraft carried the staffel's 'bomb and bow' badge on the cowling. Camouflaged in the standard RLM 74/75/76 scheme, 'Black 6' had a softly defined fuselage demarcation line with areas of diffused mottling. The cowling and wing tip undersides were yellow and the RLM 70 spinner featured a yellow tip and white band.

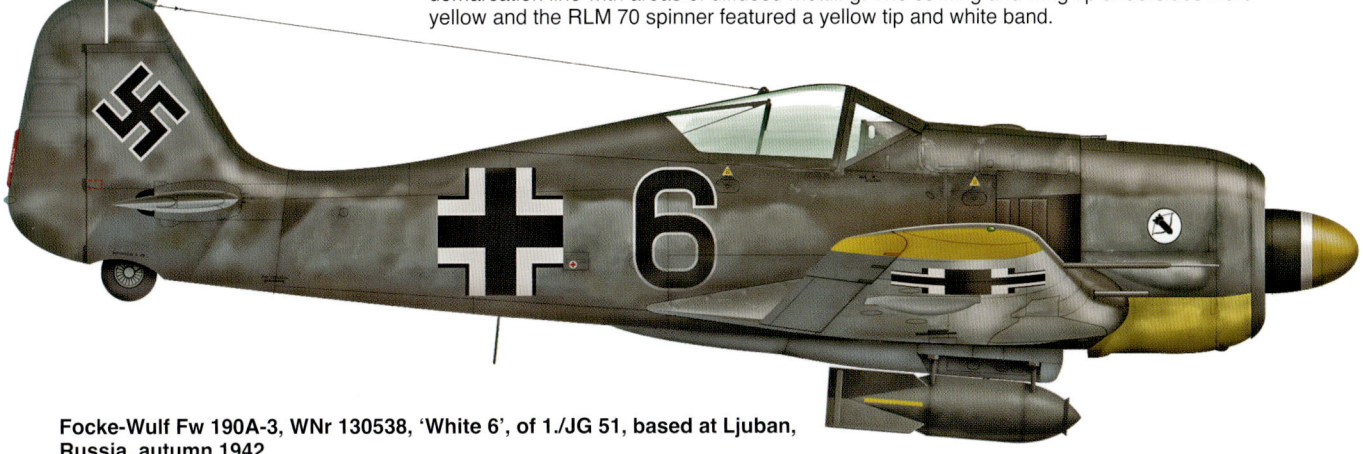

Focke-Wulf Fw 190A-3, WNr 130538, 'White 6', of 1./JG 51, based at Ljuban, Russia, autumn 1942

Involved in the invasion of the Soviet Union from the start in July 1941, initially equipped with Messerschmitt Bf 109Fs, in early September 1942, I./JG 51 was withdrawn to convert to the Fw 190. Always an innovative unit where camouflage was concerned, and with most combat operations at relatively low-level against the massed formations of ground-attack Il-2s, the Geschwader had adopted two-tone green upper surfaces for its Bf 109s, which it continued to apply when it received its new Fw 190s. These 'greens', applied in either a 'splinter' pattern or in large irregular patches or mottle, over the original RLM 74/75 'greys' were probably RLM 70 *Schwarzgrün* and RLM 71 *Dunkelgrün*, 'acquired' from bomber and transport units stationed nearby, but may have also included captured Russian paint. Yellow (RLM 04) Eastern Front Theatre, markings were also applied, in this instance in a narrow band around the rear fuselage and on the cowling underside. The last three of the werknummer '538' was retained on a patch of the original RLM 74/75/76 as was the swastika. Note the Geschwader's buzzard's head on the cowling side

Focke-Wulf Fw 190A-4, WNr 0145614, 'White 1', of Erprobungskommando 19, based at Benghazi, Libya, November 1942
Erprobungskommando 19, (EKdo 19) was a non-combat trials unit formed at Castel Benito, near Tripoli in Libya, in July 1942 equipped with a few Bf 109s and Fw 190s to test the suitability of the types for ground attack work in tropical conditions. EKdo 19 only operated for a few months and it is possible that its aircraft were transferred to operational units, as 'White 1' was found abandoned at Benghazi, Libya, some 400 miles (650km) east of Castel Benito in November 1942. The upper surfaces appear to have been overpainted with RLM 79 *Sandgelb*, and it is possible that the under surfaces and fuselage sides may also have been repainted, in the tropical scheme RLM 78 *Hellblau*. The 'last three' of the werknummer was carried on the fin tip; note also the white 'E' on the rudder which was a marking often applied to aircraft indicating they belonged to a trials unit.

Focke-Wulf Fw 190A-4, WNr 140746, 'Yellow 4', of 9./JG 2, based at Vannes, France, February 1943, flown by *Oberleutnant* Siegfried Schnell
Although the Fw 190A-4 was powered by the same BMW 801D-2 engine, and had the same armament, as the A-3, it combined all the type's developed improvements into one airframe and became the 'standard' variant for much of 1943. Fitted with a FuG 16Z radio, the aerial attachment on the fin was re-located to the top of the fin on a small stub mount – a configuration that was kept through the rest of the Fw 190's production life.
The beginning of 1943 found JG 2 in the forefront of the battle against the increasing USAAF 8th Air Force daylight bombing offensive into occupied Europe, and JG 2 was quickly re-equipped with the new variant. Finished in the standard 'mid-war greys' scheme of RLM 74/75/76, 'Yellow 4', flown by the staffelkapitän, *Oblt* Siegfried Schnell. He was awarded the Knight's Cross of the Iron Cross with Oak Leaves (*Ritterkreuz des Eisernen Kreuzes mit Eichenlaub*) after his 45th victory which was displayed, together with his subsequent victories, on the rudder. One of the top pilots in JG 2 at the time, Schnell ultimately claimed 93 aerial victories although he was officially credited with 87. He was shot down and killed in his Messerschmitt Bf 109G-6 over the Russian offensive for Narva on 25 February 1944. 'Yellow 4' had a fairly high fuselage demarcation line with restrained mottling and an area of 'discolouration' around the rear fuselage possibly covering a previously applied yellow band, maybe indicating that the aircraft had possibly been transferred from the Eastern Front. The cowling underside and rudder were painted in RLM 04 *Gelb* and the black painted exhaust-masking area featured a stylised eagle's head on the port cowling side, with the Gruppe's cockerel head on the starboard side – a regular configuration on III Gruppe machines of this period. The 'last three' of the werknummer was applied to both sides of the fin tip.

Focke-Wulf Fw 190A-4/U4, of the Stabskette, Nahaufklärungsgruppe 13, based at Dinard France, August 1943
The Fw 190A-4/U4 was a reconnaissance fighter, retaining the cowling mounted 7.92mm MG 17s and 20mm MG 151 wing root cannon and was fitted with two Rb 12.4 cameras in the rear fuselage and an EK 16 gun camera in the port wing leading edge. Nahaufklärungsgruppe 13 (NAGr 13 – Short Range Reconnaissance Wing) was formed in May 1942, in North Russia, but by August 1943, I Gruppe was based at Dinard, Brittany, northwest France, until it was moved to Chartres, southwest of Paris, following the D-Day invasion. This particular example, operated by the Geschwader Stabskette (Group Staff Flight), was finished in the standard 'mid-war greys' scheme of RLM 74/75/76 with diffused and sparse mottling on the fuselage sides which had a low colour demarcation. The cowling underside and rudder were yellow. Of note is the double chevron and short horizontal bars stab markings forward of the fuselage *balkenkreuz* and the stylised sea eagle looking over the cliffs and sea on a black-outlined shield possibly reflecting the coastal reconnaissance task of the unit.

Focke-Wulf Fw 190A-4/U8, WNr 7155, 'Yellow H' of 7./SKG 10, based at Amiens, France, spring 1943, flown by *Feldwebel* (*Fw*) Otto Bechthold
The Fw 190A-4/U8 was a long-range fighter-bomber fitted with two 300-litre drop tanks on racks mounted under the wings and a centreline ETC 501 bomb rack. The outer wing-mounted 20mm MG FF/M cannon and the cowling-mounted 7.92mm MG 17s were removed to save weight. Finished in the standard RLM 74/75/76 'mid war greys' scheme, the under surfaces, fuselage sides and fin, including the national markings, were overpainted in a temporary RLM 22 *Schwarz* black finish. On the night of 17 April 1943, due to a navigational error, *Fw* Bechtold landed at RAF West Malling, Kent and was interned. 'Yellow H' had a yellow rudder under the temporary black finish which was peeling off in places and carried a 'Schlacht' triangle in front of the fuselage *balkenkreuze*, which was also covered by the temporary black finish.

Focke-Wulf Fw 190A-4, WNr 0611, 'White 8', of 1./JG 1, based at Deelen, Netherlands, May 1943
The necessity to be able to quickly reform into staffel or Gruppe formations after a firing pass through massed USAAF heavy bomber formations, prompted attempts to develop high visibility markings for the aircraft involved. In this instance, the whole of the cowling and the spinner were painted white RLM 21 *Weiss*. Finished in the standard RLM 74/75/76 'mid-war greys' scheme, with little mottling on the fuselage sides, a random spotted finish of (possibly) RLM 76 was applied over the forward and mid-fuselage upper surfaces, and the rudder featured significant mottling. Despite being operated by 1./JG 1, the aircraft carried the 'devil in the clouds' markings of IV./JG 1 on the cowling and the 'Maltese cross shield' of III./JG 1 on the fuselage under the cockpit canopy, indicating it may have served with these units before being allocated to I./JG 1. Note that the aircraft is fitted with FuG 16ZE identified by the long aerial under the port wing.

Focke-Wulf Fw 190A-4, 'Black 2, of 2./JG 54, based in the Lake Ladoga area, Russia, early 1943
JG 54 exchanged its Messerschmitt Bf 109Fs for Focke-Wulf Fw 190A-4s in early 1943, and, like most of the Luftwaffe units operating on the Eastern Front over the winter of 1942/43, the unit applied temporary white paint over the RLM 74/75 upper surfaces of its aircraft for winter operations. Yellow Eastern Front Theatre, markings were applied 'around' the fuselage *balkenkreuze*, under the wing tips and on the cowling undersides. Note the Geschwader's famous '*Grünherz*' (Green Heart) emblem under the cockpit and I Gruppe's 'Arms of the city of Nuremberg' on the cowling. 'Black 2' is recorded as being forced down by Russian fighters on 13th January 1943 while being flown by *Unteroffizier* Helmut Brandt and was recovered by the Russians for evaluation.

Camouflage and Markings

Above:
This overhead view of Fw 190A-4, werknummer 5735, 'Black 12' of 8./JG 2 was flown by Hauptmann Bruno Stolle while based at Brest in early 1943. It displays the standard mainplane upper surface camouflage pattern with the triangular RLM 74 Dunkelgrau 'wedge-shape' on the starboard wing terminating at the aileron hinge line.

When the first Fw 190A-1s came off the production line in June 1941, contemporary photographs would appear to suggest they were finished in a contrasting two-colour upper surface scheme, similar to the '1940 scheme' of RLM 71 *Dunkelgrun* and RLM 02 *Grau*, despite the introduction and use of the 'greys scheme' on Messerschmitt Bf 109Es during the later stages of the Battle of Britain. The under surfaces were also possibly RLM 65 *Hellblau*, with a high fuselage colour demarcation.

The mottle on the fuselage sides, fin and rudder varied in style and intensity on these early Fw 190A-1s, ranging from an almost 'solid' overspray, through a distinctly 'spotty' mottle to some aircraft appearing to have no mottle applied at all! The colours in this mottling would probably have comprised RLM 70 *Schwarzgrün*, RLM 71 *Dunkelgrun* and RLM 02 *Grau* officially – but it is virtually impossible to tell from the available photos.

At least three upperwing/tailplane camouflage patterns have been identified on these early aircraft, similar to but slightly different from the later 'standard' Fw 190 pattern, although the fuselage spine pattern appears to have remained relatively constant. Later deliveries of Fw 190A-1s (Focke-Wulf AG completed 102 A-1s at the Bremen and Marienburg factories between June and late October 1941) were probably finished in the standard 'mid-war greys' of RLM 74 *Dunkelgrau/Graugrun* and RLM 75 *Mittelgrau/Grauviolett* upper surfaces with RLM 76 *Lichtblau* under surfaces and fuselage sides.

By the middle of 1942, all remaining Fw 190A-2s and the Fw 190A-3s would have been produced in the RLM 74/75/76 'greys' scheme, and throughout 1943 and up to the middle of 1944, all Luftwaffe fighters destined for the north European theatre of operations, continued to be finished in this 'mid-war greys' scheme.

By the time I./JG 26 began receiving the Fw 190A-2 during November 1941, they would almost certainly have been finished in the RLM 74/75/76 'greys' scheme, to the 'standard' Fw 190 upper surface pattern. The propeller spinners were painted the usual RLM 71 *Dunkelgrun*, although several aircraft were seen with a white quarter segment: seemingly a frequent practice. The propeller blades wore the standard RLM 70 *Schwarzgrün*.

It was during late summer/early autumn 1942, that yellow rudders and cowling undersides were first seen on Fw 190s, as tactical identification markings and an aid to rapid identification of a new type. Both the 'pale' RLM *Gelb* 27 and the 'richer' RLM *Gelb* 04 appear to have been used. An additional camouflage effect seen on several early Fw 190s was a criss-cross pattern, or undulating wavy line, along the leading edges of the mainplanes, in what appears to be RLM 71 *Dunkelgrun*.

National markings featured narrow-bordered crosses on the wing upper surfaces and broad bordered crosses on the fuselage and wing undersides. All of the crosses, or *balkenkreuze*, were outlined with narrow black borders. Even the black swastika (*hakenkreuze*) on the fin had the white border thinly outlined in black. The *werknummer*, (effectively the aircraft's serial number), often just featuring the 'last three' numerals was invariably placed on the fin top just below the aerial lead fairing, in black, in either an 'artistic European' style or plain stencil style.

Geschwader and *Gruppe Stab* chevrons and bars appear to have followed general Luftwaffe practice, although for a short period, JG 26's *Geschwaderstab* substituted the more usual chevron marking in favour of a pointed horizontal bar with what is believed to have been the first one or two letters of the pilot's surname in front, such as Fw 190A-2s coded 'S' which it is thought was flown by *Oblt* Wilfried Sieling, 'He' thought to have been flown by *Oberfeldwebel* Bruno Hegenaur and 'G' thought to have been flown by *Hauptman* Wilhelm Gäth.

Staffel numerals and *Gruppe* bars also followed general Luftwaffe practice, although 6 *Staffel* JG 26 appear to have favoured a darker colour, which may have been a shade of brown, possibly RLM 26 *Braun*.

The black-painted exhaust-masking areas seem to have been introduced on the A-2s, several aircraft serving within JG 26 and JG 2 – the second unit to be equipped with the Fw 190 from March 1942 – were recorded as having black-painted areas thinly outlined in white, over and around the exhaust slots, but it was with the introduction of the Fw 190A-3 in III/JG 2 and later the A-4 sub-type, that the stylised 'eagle's head' came to the fore.

As with most Luftwaffe aircraft, individual, *Staffel*, *Gruppe* and/or *Geschwader* badges were invariably applied on cowling sides or under the cockpit, with 'kill' markings generally applied as vertical bars, on both sides of the rudder.

The first *Jabo Staffeln*

When 10(*Jabo*)./JG 2 and 10(*Jabo*)./JG 26 re-equipped with Fw 190A-2/U3s and A-3/U3s, although they retained the standard RLM 74/75/76 'greys' scheme, with cowling undersides and rudders painted in yellow, 10(*Jabo*)./JG 2 continued to use the chevron and horizontal bar '*Jabo*' markings (introduced on the Bf 109F-4/Bs) on the rear fuselage, in the same blue shade as the numerals. The unit's brown fox with a broken ship in its jaws badge was carried on both sides of the cowling. 10(*Jabo*)./JG 26 had a different style of bar marking behind the chevron, both in black outlined in white – with the 'bar' being a stylised representation of a bomb. Numerals were also in black outlined in white.

Left:
An unidentified Fw 190A-5 obligingly sits on its nose to reveal its upper surface RLM 74/75 camouflage pattern, which was standard for the Fw 190, but note the variation on the starboard mainplane where the triangular RLM 74 Dunkelgrau 'wedge-shape' extends over the aileron hinge line all the way to the trailing edge.

Above:
Russian soldiers examining a crashed Fw 190F-8, 'Black 2' of an unidentified unit, (possibly SG 2), in early 1945 at Dombovar, Hungary. The camouflage across the fin and rudder and the black, outline-only, swastika are interesting. (Fortepan Erky-Nagy Tibor)

Eastern and Mediterranean Fronts

Ever adaptable to their surroundings, localised camouflage schemes were adopted by Luftwaffe aircraft in both the Eastern Front and Mediterranean theatres of operation. JGs 51 and 54 both opted for 'various shades of green' (and occasionally brown) upper surfaces applied at unit level over the factory 'greys' which were then changed in winter to white 'snow' upper surfaces. Similarly, some of 6./JG 2's Tunisian-based Fw 190A-4s had RLM 79 *Sandgelb* applied over their upper surfaces.

Night Fighter and specialist units

Some night fighting Fw 190s were repainted in a variety of experimental day/night schemes, before an overall RLM 76 *Hellgrau* scheme was selected.

JG 11 was especially notable for its experimental camouflage schemes designed to make their aircraft less visible in the air. Fuselage *balkenkreuze* and tail fin *hakenkreuze* were oversprayed and 'toned-down', (against regulations), almost to the point of invisibility. In addition, *Staffel* numerals were oversprayed with grey mottle, with the underside RLM 76 *Hellgrau* extending up the fuselage sides also being common.

Late war colour schemes

In mid-1944, a revised camouflage scheme was introduced for fighters, incorporating some 'new' colours within the RLM range, namely RLM 81, an olive greeny/brown shade, variously called *Braunviolett*, *Braunoliv* or *Dunkelgrün*, depending upon the amount of brown, olive or green hue in any particular paint batch; RLM 82 *Hellgrün*, a bright medium green; and RLM 83 *Dunkelgrün* a rich dark green.

These colours were used in various permutations on the upper surfaces, such as RLM 74 *Dunkelgrau* and RLM 83 *Dunkelgrün* to give a grey/green scheme, or RLM 81 *Braunviolett* and RLM 83 *Dunkelgrün* to give a brown/green scheme. RLM 82 *Hellgrün* and RLM 83 *Dunkelgrün* and to a lesser extent, RLM 81 *Braunviolett* and RLM 82 *Hellgrün* were also noted on Luftwaffe fighters. However, the previous 'mid-war' greys, RLM 74 *Dunkelgrau* and RLM 75 *Mittelgrau*, still remained a common upper surface combination right until the end of the war, although RLM 74 *Dunkelgrau* had been deleted from the RLM list of official camouflage colours. Although the basic wing and tailplane upper surface camouflage pattern essentially remained the same, there were variations in the actual demarcations, especially with the 'triangular' section on the starboard wing which sometimes, but not always, overlapped on to the aileron.

Under surface and fuselage sides remained in RLM 76 *Lichtblau*, which was prone to shade variations. For instance, the so-called 'Sky' under surfaces reported on many late-war Luftwaffe fighters including Fw 190s is now thought to be merely the result of raw material shortages and changes in the make-up of RLM 76 *Hellgrau/Lichtblau*, rather than any new RLM colour. By the later stages of the war, the percentages of pigment in the paint had decreased and was less able to cover the yellow of the zinc chromate undercoat, causing the 'colour' of RLM 76 *Lichtblau* to turn from a light blue-grey to almost a light green-grey! However, bare natural metal mainplane under surfaces with painted wing leading edges, ailerons, flaps, wing tips and various panels and access hatches were being introduced from late 1944 to speed up production and save on paint and raw materials. Mixtures of RLM 76 *Lichtblau* in the various shades including the 'Sky' hues, and bare natural metal were not uncommon by early 1945.

Mottling on the fuselage sides, cowling sides, fin and rudder appears to have been as equally open to individual manufacturers' interpretation, not to mention in-service additions, and ranged from virtually no mottle at all to a heavy dense mottle, occasionally with the cowling and/or the fin and rudder with different styles, in all probability due to dispersed manufacture and production sites, to the rest of the main fuselage. Black, or RLM 70 *Schwarzgrün*, spinners with a white spiral introduced for all Luftwaffe fighters in mid-1944 remained very common as was a black or RLM 70 *Schwarzgrün* spinner with a white 1/4 or 1/3 segment.

Balkenkreuze and *hakenkreuze* were applied in a variety of styles and sizes. Very generally speaking, upper wing crosses were white, in the 'narrow' open style, placed mid-span and showing the underlying camouflage through their 'open' centres; fuselage crosses were also invariably white, in the 'broad' open style, but often had the 'centre' filled-in with a camouflage colour and/or the white of the cross toned-down; underwing crosses were either black with broad white borders, black in a 'broad' open style, or simply a plain black cross. Swastikas could be seen in black with a white border, plain black, or an open outline style invariably in white. *Werknummern* were generally placed at the top of the fin, or occasionally mid-way down the rudder, or even at the base of the rudder (depending upon the manufacturer), sometimes with the 'last four' crudely hand-painted on the rear fuselage by the maker.

The individual aircraft numerals, applied by the unit personnel, in *Staffel* colours, were generally positioned in front of the fuselage cross, both sides, with the *Gruppe* identification symbol, a horizontal bar (II *Gruppe*), a vertical bar (III *Gruppe*), a cross or a 'squiggly' line, (IV *Gruppe*), to the rear of the fuselage cross, both sides. I *Gruppe* didn't have a *Gruppe* identification symbol, but there are examples of II, III or IV *Gruppe* aircraft failing to carry a *Gruppe* identification symbol too.

From the late 1944/early 45, until the end of World War Two, for every 'standard' scheme and marking employed there seems to have been almost as many anomalies. Force of circumstances dictated events – it was far better to have an operational fighter in the field, irrespective of whether its exterior was correctly painted or not, rather than have it lodged in a hangar awaiting the 'correct' colour scheme to be applied at some later date.

Geschwader identification bands

White and yellow rear fuselage bands had been applied to a variety of Luftwaffe aircraft, including the Fw 190, as theatre of operations markings – white for the Mediterranean Theatre and yellow for the Eastern Front, but, during the autumn of 1943, broad 'coloured bands' started to appear around the rear fuselage of some Home Defence fighter units – e.g., red bands for JG 1 and yellow bands for JG 11.

These were initially introduced at unit level, primarily as visual aids to rapid reassembly after the attacking fighters became scattered after passing through a formation of enemy bombers.

By the summer of 1944, the idea of dedicated Home Defence units was more or less academic, as most of the Luftwaffe's fighter force based on the Western and Eastern Fronts was essentially used to defend the Reich. An order from *Reichmarschall* Hermann Goering, dated 24 December 1944, instructed all *Jagdgeschwader* aircraft to be marked with coloured bands around the rear fuselage. The purpose of which was intended to improve aerial recognition, *especially* from the perspective of Axis ground troops, to better distinguish between Luftwaffe and Allied aircraft.

Each unit was allocated a different colour or combinations of colours, and a diagram illustrating the colours allocated to the various units, as they were meant to be applied to the aircraft, was issued. Bands of a single colour were to be 900mm (35.4in) wide; two colour bands were to be 550mm (21.6in) wide each; and for three bands, they were to be 300mm (11.8) wide each.

These rear fuselage bands became generally known as *Reichsverteidigung* or Defence of the Reich bands but were essentially *Geschwader* identification bands. Additional tactical markings, in the form of a yellow band around the nose and yellow rudder, introduced in March 1945 for aircraft operated by *Luftflotte* 4, were also applied at unit level and sometimes varied in width even within the same *Staffel*.

Geschwader Indentification Bands

JG 1	Bright Red
JG 2	Yellow - White - Yellow
JG 3	White
JG 4	Black - White - Black
JG 5	Black - Yellow
JG 6	Bright Red - White - Bright Red
JG 7	Blue - Red
JG 11	Yellow
JG 26	Black - White
JG 27	Bright Green
JG 51	Bright Green - White - Bright Green
JG 52	Red - White
JG 53	Black
JG 54	Bright Blue
JG 77	White - Green
JG 300	Bright Blue - White - Bright Blue
JG 301	Yellow - Red

Developing the type

Above:
Fw 190A-4, werknummer 1197, 'White 1' of 4./JG 26, flown by the Staffelkapitän, Oberleutnant Otto Stammberger, photographed in early 1943. The aircraft is in the standard 'mid-war greys' of RLM 74 Dunkelgrau and RLM 75 Mittlegrau upper surfaces with RLM 76 Lichtblau under surfaces and fuselage sides. Note the undulating fuselage demarcation line and lightly applied diffused mottling.

Right:
Another camera-equipped, photo reconnaissance Fw 190A variant, an A-4/U4, coded 'Red 6' of 5.(F)/123, based at Le Luc, France, in 1944. The Fw 190A-4/U4 was fitted with two Rb 12.4 cameras in the rear fuselage and an EK 16 or Robot II gun camera in place of the outer wing armament. Camouflage was the standard mid-war 'greys' scheme but note the distinctive mottling under the cowling and on the fin and rudder.

Building on the successes of JG 2 and JG 54's 'hit and run' tactics, a full *Geschwader* of dedicated fighter-bombers, under one unified command, was created in December 1942 and designated *SchnellKampfGeschwader 10*, (SKG 10 - Fast Bomber Wing 10).

Initially equipped with Fw 190A-4/U8s, which had the ability to carry both bombs and long range drop tanks, 10.(*Jabo*)/JG 2 and 10.(*Jabo*)/JG 54 were absorbed in to SKG 10, becoming 14./SKG 10 and 15./SKG 10 respectively, thus creating a *IV Gruppe* within the *Geschwader*.

Early in 1943, III./SKG 10 was detached to operate in the Mediterranean area, but the *Geschwader Stab*, I, II and IV *Gruppe* were retained to operate from airfields in northern France against the British mainland and coastal shipping. Operations against southern England continued from bases in the Amiens area of France until 1943, when II and IV./SKG 10 were moved to Sicily to join III./SKG 10 which was already operating

Above:
Dramatic view of an Fw 190A-4 fitted with a centreline ETC 501 bomb rack, mounted in a long streamlined ventral fairing, which had the ability to carry up to 500kg (1,100lb) of bombs or a 300-litre drop tank. The 'Jabo' retained the fuselage-mounted 7.92mm MG 17s and the wing root-mounted 20mm MG 151 cannon, but invariably deleted the outer MG-FF cannon. The inner mainwheel doors were also usually removed when the bomb rack was fitted.

Below:
Fw 190A-4 of I./JG 54 in Russia during the winter of 1942-43 with its upper surfaces covered in a temporary application of white mottle as a snow camouflage. The unit's shield denoting the arms of the City of Nuremberg is evident on the cowling.

from there. Only I./SKG 10 remained in France. Based at Dreux, the unit was by this time operating a mix of Fw 190A-4s and Fw 190A-5s.

At the beginning of April 1943, night operations using single-seat *Jabo*s had commenced. Luftwaffe High Command believed these raids to be effective and continued with them throughout the spring. Generally though, the air offensive over Britain had taken a definite turn for the worse from the Luftwaffe's perspective. Most of the Luftwaffe's bombers had been moved to the Eastern Front or elsewhere, and it was left mainly to the depleted fighter force to 'take the battle to the enemy' by both day and night. Even the 1942 'Baedekker' raids failed to achieve much beyond causing quite considerable damage to a number of British cities.

Some success was obtained by the *Jabo*s, however, when they concentrated their attacks against British coastal towns. The Chain Home radar stations continued to experience difficulty in detecting these low level raids early enough and the standing patrols of defending RAF fighters all too often failed

Left:
Fw 190A-4/U8, W/Nr 7155, 'Yellow H' of 7./SKG 10, which landed at RAF West Malling, Kent, due to a navigational error on the night of 17 April 1943. Flown by Feldwebel Otto Bechthold, who was taken prisoner, the long-range fighter-bomber had been fitted with two 300-litre drop tanks (removed prior to this photo being taken) on underwing racks and a centreline ETC 501 bomb rack, which would have carried an SC 250 kg bomb. 'Yellow H' was finished in the standard RLM 74/75/76 'mid war greys' scheme, with the under surfaces, fuselage sides and fin overpainted in a temporary black finish. (See the colour illustration section for a profile view of 'Yellow H').

to receive sufficient advance warning to make effective interceptions. Despite any successes Luftwaffe losses continued to be high, such as when, on the night of 16/17 April 1943, during a concentrated *Jabo* raid on London, eight aircraft were lost out of a force of forty-seven intruders.

Then, in the summer of 1943, just when it might be said that the effects of the nocturnal operations were starting to have an effect on British morale, they were all but terminated and reduced to nothing more than sporadic raids by individual machines. The following year, during the Allied D-Day invasion in June 1944, I./SKG 10 was practically annihilated in the attempt to stop the Allies gaining a foothold on mainland France, which effectively forced the unit to cease operations over England.

While it remains doubtful that any of the 'tip and run' raids achieved much in the way of material damage to the Allied war effort, the raids in themselves did result in a disproportionate number of defending fighters being tied down in an attempt to counter them.

Service on all Fronts

Above:
Two Fw 190A-5s of JG 54's Geschwaderstab in Russia, probably in the spring of 1943. Both are painted in various shades of green in a mix of 'semi-splinter' patches and large random mottle over the original RLM 74/75 'greys'. Additionally, the pair have yellow Eastern Front Theatre markings around their fuselages as well (we presume) as the undersides of their cowlings. The rudder on the furthest aircraft has had yellow applied to its lower portion and both aircraft wear Geschwader Kommodore stab markings.

Right:
A line up of 5./SG 1's Fw 190A-5/U3s at Deblin-Irena in the spring of 1943. Points of interest are the Gruppe badge on the cowling of the aircraft in the foreground – a pistol and hatchet-wielding Mickey Mouse on a red disc – and a black and red spinner smartly divided by a thin white line.

Night Fighter A-5

The A-5 was the first Fw 190 sub-type to be adapted for night fighting. On 24 July 1943 RAF bombers attacked Hamburg and successfully jammed German radar equipment with the aid of 'Window' – tiny strips of metal foil cut to pre-determined length. The raid prompted the German High Command to give greater urgency to *Oberst* Hajo Herrmann's proposals, then being tested, to attack the bombers visually using single-engined fighters operating with the aid of searchlights or the light from flares. This method of attack, in which the night fighters operated independently of radar, was known as *'Wilde Sau'* (Wild Boar). As insufficient numbers of fighters were available to set up dedicated single-engine *Nachtjagd* (night fighter) units, II./JG 1 hosted elements of *'Jagdgruppe Herrmann'* and also undertook night sorties against British bombers.

Although successful during the light

summer nights, Herrmann's *'Wilde Sau'* units began to suffer heavy losses with the onset of winter, and in order to minimise them several Fw 190s were fitted with FuG 217 *Neptun* (Neptune) radar sets. Day and night sorties were flown from July through to September 1943, but pilot fatigue was a major cause

Above:
Another photo of 5./SG 1's Fw 190A-5/U3s lined up at Deblin-Irena in the spring of 1943. The aircraft are newly delivered and look very clean; each is finished in the standard RLM 74/75/76 'greys' scheme. They carry red letters outlined in white in front of the fuselage balkenkreuze (cross) and a black and white Schlacht triangle behind. Several airframes have yet to receive their distinctive gun-and-hatchet toting Mickey Mouse Gruppe badge, although all appear to have had their spinners appropriately painted in black, white and red.

Right:
Fw 190A-5/U3 'Black 4' of 10.(Jabo)/JG 54, taxiing out at its based at St Omer-Wizernes, France, in early 1943 for another low-level strike against British coastal towns. In February 1943, 10.(Jabo)/JG 26 became 10.(Jabo)/JG 54 but continued to operate under the control of JG 26. The unit continued to use the stylised 'bomb' design aft of the chevron as its 'Jabo' marking. Cowling underside and rudder were yellow and the aircraft appears to be carrying a 500kg bomb on its ETC 501 centreline rack.

of attrition and the experiment was ultimately abandoned. The A5/R11 was a night fighter conversion fitted with *Neptun* with arrays of three dipole aerials vertically mounted fore and aft of the cockpit and above and below the wings, while flame-damper shields were fitted over the exhaust louvres. These A-5/R-11s were operated by II./JG 300 in late 1943/early 1944.

Approximately 1,752 A-5s were built from November 1942 to June 1943.

Below:
Luftwaffe ground crew pose in front of an Fw 190A-5/R1 of 10 Staffel, IV./JG 1 at Bergen-op-Zoom or Deelen in the summer of 1943. This aircraft was fitted with FuG 16ZY an airborne VHF transceiver used in single-seat fighters for R/T communications, and also for Y-Verfarhren (Y-Control), in which aircraft operated as Leitjäger (Fighter Formation Leaders) that could be tracked and directed from the ground. Aircraft equipped with FuG 16ZY were fitted with a Morane aerial which can be seen under the port wing. Also of interest is the IV Gruppe 'circle' symbol aft of the fuselage cross and what is thought to be a yellow underside to the cowling.

Above:
One of many Luftwaffe aircraft left in Tunisia when the Germans evacuated the country in early May 1943, this Fw 190A-5/U3, W/Nr 152676 of III./SKG 10, being inspected by American pilots, was abandoned at El Aouina airfield. An example of a replacement machine rushed into service with its factory codes KM+EY still in place, it is finished in the standard RLM 74/75/76 'greys' scheme. The aircraft has the Mediterranean Theatre white rear fuselage band applied. (HMP)

Below:
Fw 190A-5/U14, W/Nr 871, TD+SI, the first of two A-5/U14 torpedo bomber prototypes. Finished in the standard RLM 74/75/76 scheme, the aircraft had strengthened undercarriage, extended tailwheel leg and enlarged fin and rudder. It is photographed carrying an LTF 5b torpedo.

Focke-Wulf Fw 190A-5, 'White 11, of 1./JG 54, based at Nicolskoye, Russia, summer 1943

During the summer of 1943, JG 54 one of the most successful fighter units in the Luftwaffe, was starting to re-equip with the Fw 190A-5 operating in the air superiority role. Originally finished in the standard factory RLM 74/75 upper surfaces 'White 11' has been overpainted in a field-applied meander scheme of browns and greens; possibly RLM 81 *Dunkelgrün*, RLM 81a *Olivbraun* and RLM 82 *Dunkelgrün*, or a mix of Luftwaffe and Russian colours. It should also be noted that at this time, RLM 81, 81a and 82 were not officially in service and there is some debate that JG 54 was perhaps chosen as a trial unit for the new colours. Standard yellow Eastern Front Theatre markings were carried 'around' the fuselage *balkenkreuze* and under the wing tips, plus on the cowling underside and the lower portion of the rudder. Again, the Geschwader's famous '*Grünherz*' (Green Heart) emblem was applied under the cockpit and I Gruppe's 'Arms of the city of Nuremberg' on the cowling.

Focke-Wulf Fw 190A-5, WNr 1197, 'White 1' of 4./JG 26, based at Abbeville Drucat, France, May 1943, flown by the Staffelkapitän, *Oberleutnant* Otto Stammberger

By the beginning of 1943, JG 26 together with elements of JG 1, JG 2, JG 51 and JG 52, were bearing the brunt of allied operations over France and the Low Countries (although I./JG 26 and 7 Staffel were temporarily transferred to the Eastern Front they had returned by the summer). *Oberleutnant* Otto Stammberger, Staffelkapitän of 4./JG 26, was shot down by Spitfires near St Omer in 'White 1' and although he bailed out, his parachute only partially opened and he was knocked unconscious upon hitting the ground. Although he recovered, he was transferred to 2./JGr West based at Biaritz in France, where on 31 December 1943, he was credited with a USAAF B-17 shot down near Bergerac – his seventh, and last, victory.

Finished in the standard RLM 74/75/76 'mid-war greys' scheme, there appeared to be very little mottling on the fuselage sides and fin of 'White 1' while the cowling underside and rudder were painted in the Channel Front RLM 04 *Gelb*.

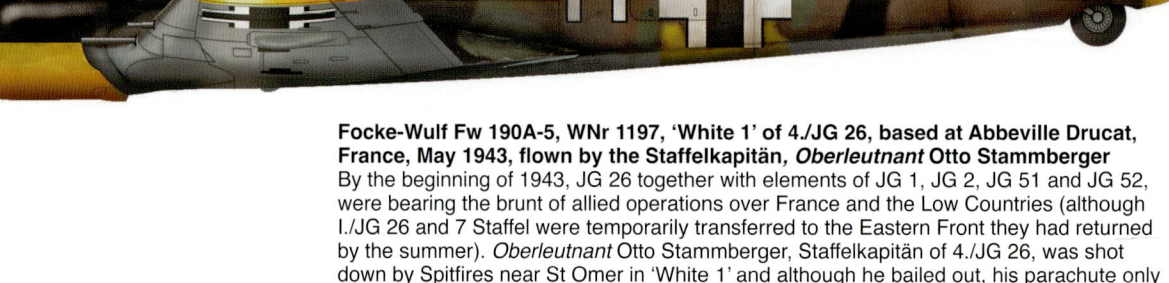

Focke-Wulf Fw 190A-5/U12, WNr 410266, 'Black 13' of 2./JG 11, based at Husum, Germany, autumn 1943, flown by the Staffelkapitän, *Leutnant* Erich Hondt

The *Umrüstbausätz* 12 designation, comprising a pair of 20mm 151/20 cannon in WB (Waffen-Behälter) pods under the wings, was combat tested by 2./JG 11 in the autumn of 1943 and although its operational use was restricted, it was subsequently provided as a *Rüstsätz* (in-the-field kit), under the designation R1, and fitted to Fw 190A-6s, A-7s and A-8s. Following the experiments with high-visibility markings earlier in the summer, the units involved in defending the Reich from the growing USAAF bomber formations, introduced other rapid identification markings, including a red diagonal Schwarmführer band along the forward fuselage sides (which appeared as a 'V' from above), and Staffelkapitäne often had their aircraft's empennage painted white, both of which are illustrated here on 'Black 13', flown by 2 Staffel's, Staffelkapitän *Leutnant* Erich Hondt who was ultimately credited with at least 10 victories. Finished in the standard 'mid war greys' scheme, the cowling underside was yellow and the spinner is thought to have been RLM 23 *Rot* (red), although it may have been finished in a solid coat of RLM 70. Note the 2 Staffel emblem, a pixie defecating into Uncle Sam's hat, on the cowling, inherited from 8./JG 3 when that unit was redesignated in the summer of 1943.

Focke-Wulf Fw 190A-5/R6, WNr 181729, 'White 42' of Erprobungskommando 25, based at Wittmund, Germany, May 1943

Erprobungskommando 25 was formed May 1943 in Wittmund in Germany, with a Stab and 1, 2 and 3 Staffeln, to test special weapons and develop anti-day bomber tactics, before moving to Achmer in the September. Amongst the first anti-bomber weapons tested, the air-to-air Wfr.Gr 21 (*Werfer-Granate* 21) rocket launcher, under the *Rüstsätz* modification kit designation R6, was designed to break up USAAF bomber 'box formations'. 'White 42', possibly of 1./Ekdo 25, was finished in the standard RLM 74/75/76 'mid-war greys' scheme, and apart from the large white numeral '42' thinly outlined in black, carried no other markings, with the exception of the JG 2-style black painted exhaust-masking area and the WNr on the fin tip. The RLM 70 spinner was quartered with white. Note the non-standard style of the '4'.

Focke-Wulf Fw 190A-5, D5+XV of 10./NJG 3, based at Aalborg-West, Denmark, early 1944

Nachtjagdgeschwader 3 was a dedicated night fighter unit formed in September 1941, mainly equipped with Bf 110s and later with Ju 88s and Do 217s. IV Gruppe was formed in November 1942, with 10 Staffel detached to Aalborg-West and partially equipped with Fw 190A-5s. Camouflaged in a variation of the 'mid war greys' scheme, the aircraft carries a lower 'solid' fuselage demarcation. D5+XV also carried the Geschwader's four digit codes. The small 'D5' unit designator in front of the fuselage *balkenkreuz*, (which appears to be the 'open' white only style, as does the swastika), being the code for NJG 3, the 'X' the aircraft's individual identification letter. The 'V' denotes 10 Staffel. The aircraft also carries the famous '*Englandblitz*' emblem on the cowl. This marking was adopted by the Nachtjagdgeschwader, and was designed by Victor Mölders, brother of Werner Mölders, when he was attached to 1./ZG 1.

Focke-Wulf Fw 190A-6, WNr 550445, 'Green 1' of Stab JG Herrmann, based at Bonn/Hangelar, Germany, 1943

The Fw 190A-6 was developed to improve the type's ability to attack USAAF heavy bombers, and this particular example, was flown by *Major* Hans-Joachim 'Hajo' Herrmann, a successful bomber pilot, who was appointed to the Luftwaffe Operational Staff and in mid-1943, played a role in the creation of Jagdgeschwader 300 '*Wilde Sau*' (Wild Boar) using 'free roaming' Fw 190 day fighters at night, flown by experienced night fighter pilots and ex-instructors, to combat RAF Bomber Command raids on Germany. Hermann himself flew more than 50 '*Wilde Sau*' missions, claimed nine victories, and was twice forced to bail out of his stricken fighter. Finished in the standard day-fighter scheme of RLM 74/75/76 scheme, 'Green 1' is illustrated with seven victory tabs on the rudder.

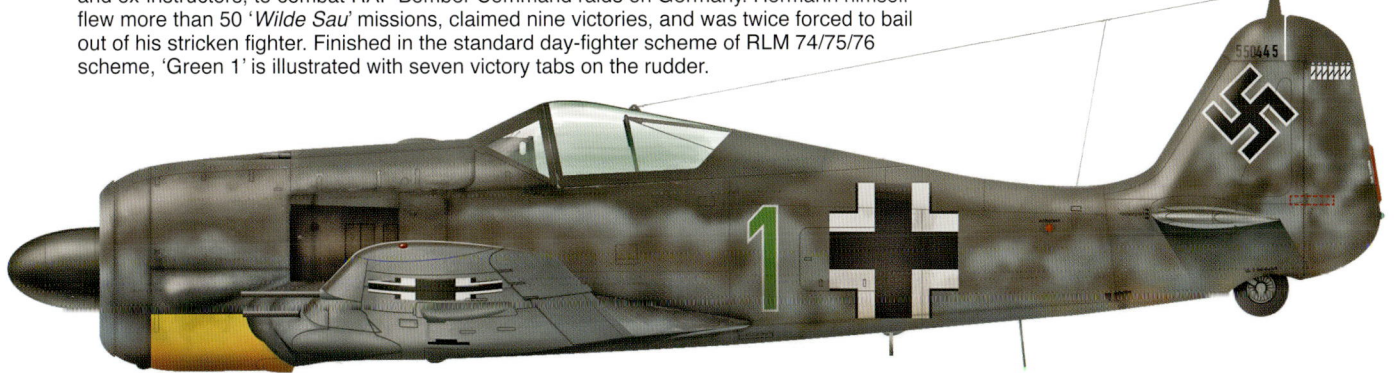

Focke-Wulf Fw 190A-6, WNr 550490, 'White 5' of 1./JG 1, based at Deelen, Netherlands, October 1943, flown by *Unteroffizier* Rudolf Hübl

By October 1943, JG 1 was primarily tasked with Defence of the Reich (*Reichsverteidigung*) operations. As such, JG 1 continued experimenting with painting their aircraft cowlings for rapid identification – in this case with black and white checks as illustrated by 'White 5', or broad horizontal stripes. 'White 5' was finished in the standard RLM 74/75/76 scheme and retained the yellow cowling underside. The spinner was white with a black spiral. The WNr was applied to the fin tip and the four 'kill' tabs on the rudder represent three USAAF B-17s and an RAF P-51 Mustang.

Focke-Wulf Fw 190A-6, of Stab II./JG 54, based at Immola, Russia, June 1944, flown by the Gruppenkommandeur, *Major* Erich Rudorffer

In July 1943, following his service with JG 2 in Tunisia and Sicily, *Hauptmann* Rudorffer was appointed to command II./JG 54, which was based on the Eastern Front. He claimed his first victory there on 7 August and achieved incredible success. During his first sortie on 24 August 1943, he downed five Soviet aircraft in four minutes and on 11 October 1943 he entered the history books when he claimed thirteen 'kills' in seventeen minutes. The Fw 190A-6 he flew in the summer of 1944, sporting the 'double chevron' of the Gruppenkommandeur and horizontal II Gruppe bar, was finished in the standard RLM 74/75/76 'greys' scheme, with fairly dense mottling along the fuselage sides. The aircraft had the Eastern Front yellow Theatre markings 'behind' the fuselage *balkenkreuze*, under the wing tips and on the lower portion of the rudder. The colour applied to the cowling underside is open to speculation and may have been a shade of green, such as RLM 71, as illustrated here. Note the broad black spiral on the spinner.

Focke-Wulf Fw 190A-6, 'White 2' of Sturmstaffel 1, based at Dortmund, Germany, January 1944

The origin of *sturm* tactics, (a contraction of '*sturmbock*' – battering ram) can be traced back to *Reichsmarschall* Hermann Goering's insistence that Reich Defence units should start ramming USAAF bombers as a last resort! *Major* Hans-Georg von Kornatzki formed a test unit, Sturmstaffel 1, in which the staffel members pledged 'not to open fire on the bombers until 150-200 metres away, and if the gunfire was ineffective, to ram the bomber'. Finished in the standard RLM 74/75/76 'greys' scheme with a yellow cowling underside, 'White 7' also had black-white-black banding around the rear fuselage, which pre-dated the so-called *Reichsverteidigung* (Reich Defence) bands, (essentially Geschwader identification bands) introduced at the end of 1944. Note the gauntlet holding a lightning bolt staffel badge on the cowling side and the additional armour around the cockpit area and reinforced canopy.

Colour Profiles

Focke-Wulf Fw 190A-7, 'Black 3' of 2./JG 1, based at Dortmund, Germany, January 1944

Based alongside Sturmstaffel 1 at Dortmund, I./JG1 were amongst the first recipients of the Fw 190A-7, production of which began in late 1943. Powered by the same BMW 801D-2 engine the sub-type's basic armament was somewhat enhanced by replacing the cowling-mounted 7.9mm MG 17s with two 13mm MG 131s which now required faired bulges to accommodate their larger breeches. The three cowling toggle latches were also relocated, to the side panels. The rest of the armament fit stayed the same as earlier versions with two wing root and two outer wing 20mm MG 151/20E cannon. Like JG 11, JG 1 also experimented with painting their aircraft's cowlings, in this instance with broad black and white horizontal stripes, as illustrated by 'Black 3'. Finished in the standard RLM 74/75/76 scheme, with little or no mottling on the fuselage sides, it retained the yellow cowling underside. JG 1 was allocated a broad red Geschwader identification band; note how the rear edge of which followed the tail unit transportation join. Some profiles depict a WNr carried on the fin, but photographic evidence shows this not to be present.

Focke-Wulf Fw 190A-8/R2, 'Black 13' of 11.(Sturm)/JG 3, based at Schongau, Germany, August 1944, flown by *Leutnant* Werner Gerth

On the Fw 190A-8/R2 the outer wing 20mm cannon were replaced with 30mm MK 108 cannon, making the sub-type a much heavier aircraft. This virtually doubled the fuel consumption rate making the carriage of a centreline 300-litre drop tank a virtual necessity – further adding to the weight of the aircraft. Few pilots resorted to actually ramming a bomber unless they had the chance of escaping safely, but *Leutnant* Gerth, Staffelkapitän of 11 Staffel, who was shot down at least eleven times, was finally killed when his parachute failed to open after ramming a B-17 near Halle. Finished in the standard RLM 74/75/76 scheme, the fuselage sides appear to have been darkened, possibly with field-mixed paint, leaving the original finish around the fuselage cross. 'Black 13' featured the black cowling and the Geschwader's 'winged U' shield, which was embellished by a black exhaust-masking area, possibly outlined in white (as illustrated) or yellow. The broad white Geschwader identification band was applied, over which a truncated wavy line variation of the IV Gruppe identification marking was painted. The spinner was black with a white spiral.

Focke-Wulf Fw 190A-8/R2, WNr 681497, 'White 11' of 5.(Sturm)/JG 4, based at Babenhausen, Germany, January 1945, flown by *Gefreiter* Walter Wagner

Jagdgeschwader 4 was one of the three Jagdgeschwader to operate specialised Sturmgruppen. II.(Sturm)/JG 4 was formed on 12 July 1944 at Salzwedel from I./ZG 1 and elements of Sturmstaffel 1 and equipped with the heavily armoured Fw 190A-8/R2, fitted with 5mm appliqué plates of armour sheet to protect the cockpit area and engine. Flown on Operation 'Bodenplatte' on 1 January 1945, 'White 11' made a forced landing at St Trond, Belgium. Later repaired it was flown by American pilots from the 404th FG. Finished in the mid-war 'greys scheme, with weathered and overpainted areas in different shades, the port cowling carried a knight's helmet with a white plume on a blue shield, first used by II Gruppe, but which later also appeared on other JG 4 aircraft, with red or white plumes. In common with other fighter units engaged in *Reichsverteidigung* operations, JG 4 had Geschwader identification bands applied to its aircraft, in JG 4's case a black-white-black band, presumably inherited from Sturmstaffel 1. Again, the spinner had a white spiral. Note the small areas of primer applied to the fuselage armour plate and undercarriage door.

Focke-Wulf Fw 190A-8/R6, 'Black 8' of 3./JGr 10, based at Parchim, Germany, early 1945

A semi-autonomous 'trials' unit, formed in July 1944, from Erprobungskommando 25, itself an experimental test and evaluation unit, Jagdgruppe 10 comprised of the Stab and three staffeln, 1, 2 and 3./JGr 10, of which 2 and 3 Staffeln were the 'operational' aspect of the Gruppe, whilst 1 Staffel undertook the experimental trials work and trained the pilots. Stationed at Parchim during the summer and autumn of 1944, the staffel's aircraft were fitted with a *Rüstsätz* 6 (R6) Wfr.Gr 21 (*Werfer-Granate* 21), 21cm mortar tube under each wing. Camouflaged in the standard RLM 74/75/76 'greys' scheme, the unit had a mix of fighter-style black individual aircraft codes outlined in red forward of the fuselage *balkenkreuz*, and unit identification code 'I1' (in small characters) to the rear. Added to this was a very distinctive and 'different' red and yellow snake design which was painted along the length of the fuselage. Also of note is the numeral '3' applied to the exhaust shield. Placed under the operational command of II.(Sturm)/JG 300, 3./JGr 10 was essentially operated as the Sturm unit's 8 Staffel, following the order to expand the JG 300 in to a four-staffeln Gruppen in mid-July 1944. The unit was disbanded March 1945.

Focke-Wulf Fw 190A-8, 'Blue 8' 'Erika' of 12./JG 5, based at Herdla, Norway, early 1945,

Towards the end of 1944, each of JG 5's Gruppen were expanded into four staffeln, which caused the renumbering of II, III and IV's existing staffeln to accommodate the new fourth unit. Then, in early January 1945, IV Gruppe was completely re-equipped with the Bf 109G-14, resulting in the Fw 190A-7s and A-8s being re-allocated to III Gruppe, with 'Blue 8' being allocated to the 'new' 12 Staffel, which explains the retention of the IV Gruppe blue numerals and disc marking. Finished in the mid-war 'greys' scheme, 'Blue 8' sported a blue and white spinner with a black spiral, superimposed, and a blue armoured cowling ring. A shield with a red sun setting over an arctic sea and the word '*Eismeer*' (arctic sea) was applied to the cowling and appears to have only been used on the Fw 190A-8s of III Gruppe in April/May 1945.

Focke-Wulf Fw 190A-9/R11, WNr 490044, 'Red 22' of 6./JG 301, found abandoned at Langensalza, Germany, May 1945

The Fw 190A-9 was essentially the final model of the A-series, production of which started in the autumn of 1944 and continued in parallel with the A-8 variant. Powered by a BMW 801S engine, the sub-type was invariably fitted with the FuG 125 radio and PKS 12 radio direction finder equipment (under the *Rüstsätz* 11 numbering system) and a 'blown' canopy hood. In the last few months of World War Two, II./JG 301 operated a mix of Fw 190 A-8s and A-9s, 'Red 22' being an A-9/R11. The aircraft was finished in the mid-war 'greys scheme with diffused mottling on the fuselage sides, fin and rudder. Featuring JG 301's yellow and red Geschwader identification band, upon which a red (thinly outlined in white) II Gruppe horizontal bar has been painted, the unusually high individual aircraft number '22' was red without any outline. Late-war style black outline crosses and plain black swastika were carried, with the werknummer on the fin tip, and a white spiral on the spinner.

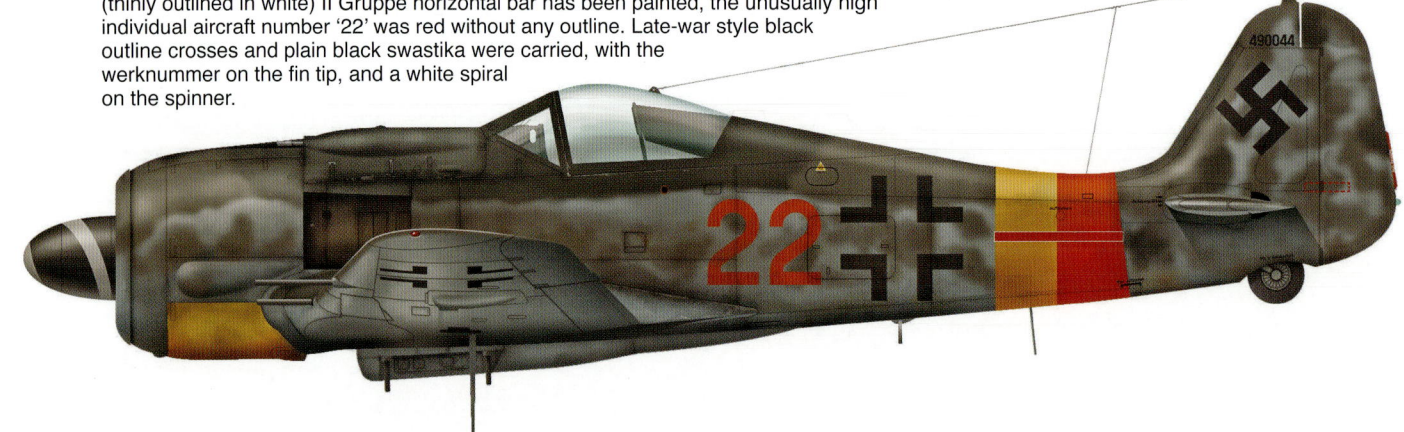

Focke-Wulf Fw 190F-3/R1 'White M' of 4./SG 5, based at Pontsalemjoki, Finland, early 1944
The Fw 190F series was developed as a dedicated 'ground attack' version. Additional armour was added to the underside of the fuselage protecting the fuel tanks, pilot, and engine. The most common version of the F-3, (based upon the Fw 190A-5), was the F-3/R1, as illustrated here, which, in addition to the ETC 501 centreline bomb rack, which could carry a 250kg bomb (illustrated), 500kg bomb, or up to eight SC 50 50kg bombs on an ER 4 adaptor, had the wing outer gun positions removed and two ETC 50 bomb racks fitted under each wing for SC 50 bombs. 4 Staffel of Schlachtgeschwader 5 (4./SG 5) was formed in February 1944 in Petsamo from 14.(*Jabo*)/JG 5 but by May 1944 was re-designated 1./SG 5. The aircraft featured here, 'White M', was finished in the standard mid-war 'greys' scheme, with 'splinter' segments of white over the upper surfaces for 'snow' camouflage. The aircraft carried no unit or personal emblems but had a yellow band around the rear fuselage, yellow cowling underside and a white tip to the RLM 70 spinner.

Focke-Wulf Fw 190F-8, 'White 1' of 1./SG 4, based at Jakobstadt, Latvia, July 1944.
Following its re-formation into Schlachtgeschwader 4 in October 1943 from elements of II./SchG 2, I./SG 4 continued to operate in the ground attack role in Italy until July 1944 when the Gruppe was transferred to the Eastern Front. Still finished in a unit-applied Mediterranean Theatre camouflage of RLM 79 *Sandgelb* with RLM 80 *Olivgrün* mottling, which had been crudely painted over the factory-applied RLM 74/75 upper surface scheme and around the national markings and completely over the swastika on the fin. 'White 1' retained its white wing tip under surfaces and rear fuselage band, the upper part of which was overpainted, and had a yellow cowling underside. I./SG 4's axe-wielding Mickey Mouse riding a green bomb which was adopted by the unit from II./SchG 2 and displayed on the cowling. The RLM 70 spinner carries a white spiral.

Focke-Wulf Fw 190F-8/R1, 'Green 2' of Stab I./SG 2, based at Papa, Hungary, January 1945
Schlachtgeschwader 2 was another ground attack/close-support unit that had originally been equipped with Ju 87s, principally based in the southern sector of the Eastern Front. Whilst II./SG 2, (formerly II./SchG 1), had been equipped with the Fw 190 since late 1942, I./SG 2 was only converted in June 1944. As one of only two Fw 190-equipped ground attack Geschwader on the Eastern Front, SG 2 was heavily committed during 1944, and, as in previous winters on the Eastern Front, a white winter finish was somewhat hastily field-applied in a 'wave mirror' design over the standard RLM 74/75 scheme upper surfaces. Under surfaces remained in RLM 76 *Hellgrau*. A narrower than usual yellow Eastern Front recognition band was applied around the fuselage just to the rear of the cross and the cowling underside tray was also yellow. The armoured ring and cowling front was painted in the Stab colour of green and the aircraft also sported the yellow 'V' under the port wing applied to aircraft operating in Hungary. Note the truncated aircraft code, 'blown' canopy hood and the AB 500 munitions container on the ETC 501 rack which when released, opened to drop six SD 2 anti-tank bombs.

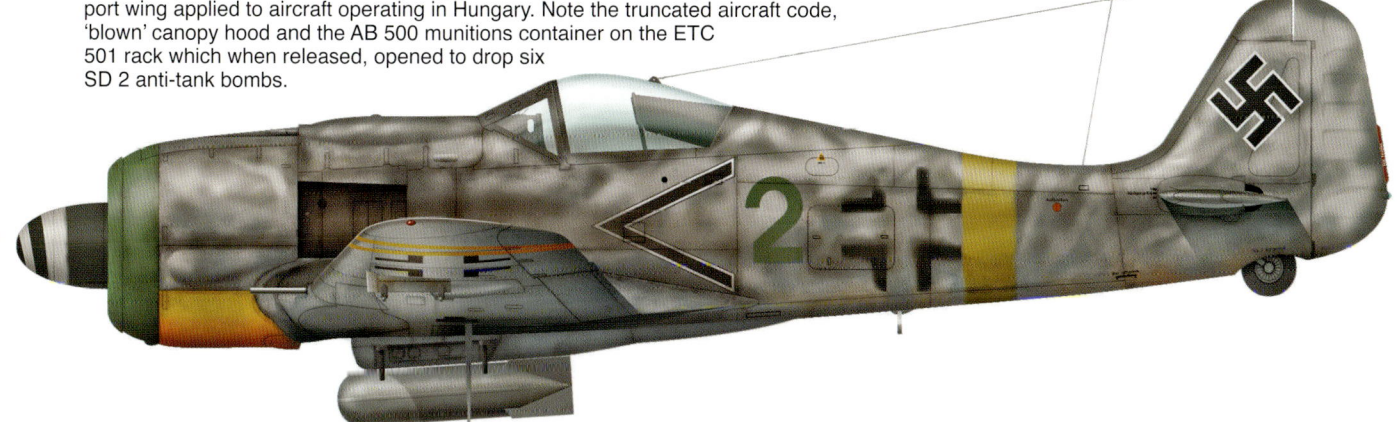

Focke-Wulf Fw 190F-8, 'Black 11' attached to 5./SG 77, based at Pardubice, Protectorate of Bohemia & Moravia, March 1945

II Gruppe Schlachtgeschwader 77, a close air support/ground attack unit, was formed in October 1943 from a mix of elements from SchG 1, SchG 2 and SG 4 and equipped with Fw 190Fs from the start. 'Black 11' was finished in the standard RLM 74/75/76 'greys' scheme, with diffused mottling along the fuselage sides, fin and rudder. No specific Schlacht markings were carried, just a black numeral '11' outlined in white and a plain black II Gruppe, horizontal bar behind the fuselage *balkenkreuze*. No unit badges have been applied but there is a red 'lightning arrow' on the cowling and the remnants of yellow around the armoured cowling ring. The aircraft is illustrated armed with Panzerschreck 1, (Flying Tank Terror), comprising three metal tubes welded together, mounted on the four underwing ETC 71 racks, firing 88mm bulged hollow-charge warhead anti-tank rockets.

Focke-Wulf Fw 190F-8, WNr 681330, 'Yellow 11' II.(Sturm)/SG 2, based at Neubiberg, Germany, March 1945

Perhaps reflecting the chaotic nature of the last few weeks of World War Two for the Luftwaffe, this particular Fw 190F-8 appears to have had its original 8 Staffel/III Gruppe red numeral and vertical bar markings overpainted with 6 Staffel/II Gruppe yellow numeral and horizontal bar markings indicating a hurried change of Staffel and Gruppe, and perhaps even Geschwader. Finished in the RLM 74/75/76 scheme, the aircraft features a yellow rudder and front to the cowling, introduced in March 1945 as tactical identification markings for aircraft operated by Luftflotte 4, although officially it should have been a 500mm wide band around the cowling. Note the late-war 'open' style fuselage cross and swastika, and the aircraft's werknummer across the fin and rudder is interestingly applied in a non-standard stencilled style.

Focke-Wulf Fw 190S-8, 'Red 55' of an unidentified unit, captured by Allied troops at Flensburg, Germany, 1945

As the Luftwaffe phased out the Ju 87 in the ground attack role and replaced it with the Fw 190, there was a need to train Ju 87 pilots to operate the Fw 190. Pilots needed to make the transition as quickly and smoothly as possible and thus was born the training version of the Fw 190. Initially, several 'old' Fw 190A-5s were converted by replacing the MW 50 water-methanol tank with a second cockpit, however, later in 1944, Fw 190A-8s were modified. Originally known as Fw 190A-8/U1s, the twin-seater trainers were re-designated as Fw 190S-8s. As several damaged airframes from frontline units were also modified, it is difficult to determine a precise number of A-5s and A-8s that were converted to become two-seater trainers, but it was probably no more than 60 or so. At least two of the Luftwaffe's seven *Jagdfliegerschulen* (JFS or Fighter Pilot Schools), JFS 2 and JFS 5, operated twin-seat Fw 190s, and this particular example is based on an Fw 190F-8 that was captured by Allied troops at Flensburg, Germany in 1945. Finished in the standard mid-war 'greys' scheme, 'Red 55' was fitted with the original/earlier style rear canopy of the A-5 two-seat variant, which could have been a replacement.

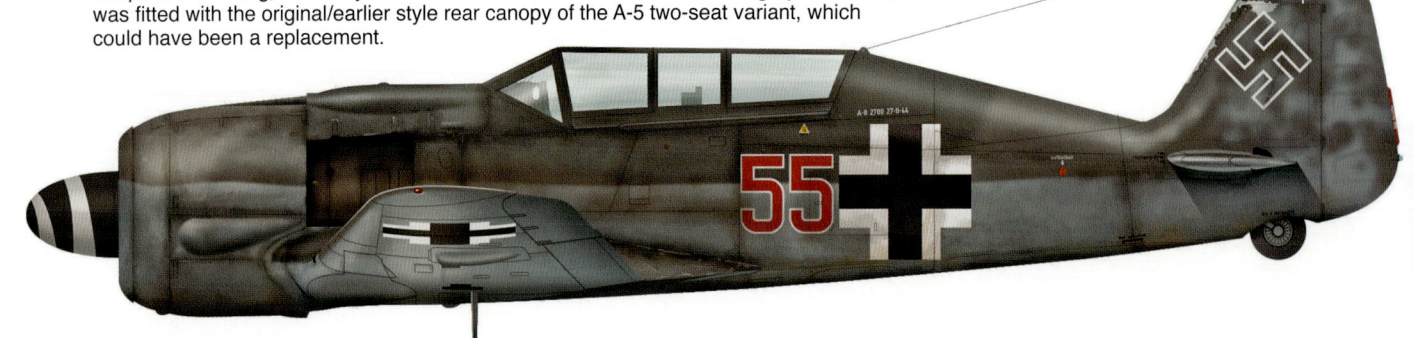

Focke-Wulf Fw 190Aa-3, 'Black 37', 5th Fighter Regiment, *Türk Hava Kuvvetleri* (Turkish Air Force), Eskisehir airbase, Turkey, circa mid-1940s

In the summer of 1942, Germany exported approximately 72 Fw 190As to Turkey in exchange for chromium and high-grade iron badly needed by German manufacturing industries. In essence, the exported airframes were Fw 190A-3s now designated as Fw 190Aa-3s, (the lower case 'a' standing for *auslandisch* [foreign]). The aircraft were powered by BMW 801D-2 engines, had FuG VIIa radios and an armament of four MG 17 7.92mm machine guns – two in the cowling and one each in the outboard wing position – with the option of installing two MG-FF 20mm cannon in the outer wing positions in lieu of the MG 17s. The export order was completed between October 1942 and March 1943 and the Fw 190Aa-3s remained in Turkish service until late 1947 when they were retired due to a lack of spare parts. Initially delivered in the Luftwaffe RLM 74/74/76 scheme and Turkish markings, 'Black 37' appears to have either a repainted or replacement empennage with a different camouflage pattern, possibly in RAF Dark Earth and Dark Green with Sky Blue under surfaces (as illustrated). The engine cowling may also have been a replacement. The 5th Fighter Regiment comprised four *Filos* (squadrons), named '*Sarybas*', '*Karabas*', '*Albas*' and '*Akbas*' with the propeller spinners painted in individual *Filo* identification colours.

Focke-Wulf Fw 190A-4, WNr 0142 308, of III./SKG 10, La Marsa, Tunis, May 1943

This particular Fw 190A-4 was captured at Sidi Ahmed, and after repair, flown to La Marsa by Sqn/Ldr Bobby Oxspring for evaluation. Finished in the standard RLM 74/75/76 scheme with densely mottled fuselage sides, the white Mediterranean Theatre rear fuselage band had been partially overpainted along the spine although the wing tip underside colours remained unchanged. It had its Luftwaffe markings crudely overpainted in 'squares' of blue on the wing upper and under surfaces, and over the swastika which then had red and white stripes superimposed. The fuselage crosses had red, white and blue stripes applied over them. The cowling underside tray was yellow and the propeller spinner in the standard RLM 70 *Schwarzgrün*. The aircraft was test flown on a number of occasions, but its ultimate fate is unknown.

Focke-Wulf Fw 190A-5/Trop, captured by the 85th Fighter Squadron 'Flying Skulls' 79th Fighter Group, USAAF, based at Gerbini, Sicily in August 1943

This Fw 190A-5 (werknummer unknown) was one of three Fw 190s originally captured in Tunisia by the 85th Fighter Squadron 'Flying Skulls', 79th Fighter Group, USAAF, (two Fw 190A-5s and a G-3) and restored to flying standard. All the Fw 190s were repainted, and crews were given a fairly wide scope of artistic licence! This one had a particularly gaudy scheme applied and shows evidence of several repaints or additions to the scheme. It should be noted that the following assumptions are based on interpretation of wartime black and white photographs and eye-witness notes, so is open to speculation. Comprising what are possibly Insignia Red 45 fuselage upper surfaces extending on to the wing roots, the forward section is quite heavily weathered and possibly displays areas of faded Olive Drab 41. The spinner was probably red with areas of Olive Drab paint visible. Both surfaces of the wings and tailplane look to be finished in Identification Yellow 48, with red tips. The fuselage undersides are also estimated to be in yellow, along with the fuselage band, although this appears to have been overpainted with a colour similar to either Sand 49 (or ANA 616) or RAF Mid Stone, along with areas of yellow left exposed. USAAF national markings were applied in all six positions and red, white and blue horizontal stripes were painted on the rudder. The 85th FS's 'Flying Skull' insignia was applied to both sides of the aircraft which was fitted with tropical air filters. This Fw 190A-5 was later flown by the Fighter Training School at Constantine, Algeria.

Fighters and Ground Attack

Fw 190A-6

The Fw 190A-6 was developed to improve the type's ability for attacking USAAF heavy bombers. The *Umrüstbausätz* and *Rüstsätz* kit modifications had caused the weight of the Fw 190 to creep up and to combat this and allow better weapons to be installed in the wings, a structurally redesigned and lighter wing was introduced. Standard armament remained

Pages 52 - 55:

A series of photos taken of Fw 190A-6s of II./JG 54. Part of Detachment Kuhlmey, based at Immola, Finland, in the summer of 1944, it was commanded by Oberstleutnant Kurt Kuhlmey and comprised a mixed force of some seventy aircraft including Ju 87Ds of I./SG 3; Fw 190Fs of I./SG 5; Bf 109G-8s of I./NaGr 5, and the Fw 190A-6s of II./JG 54.

Fighters and Ground Attack

Left hand page top:
Ground crew work on Fw 190A-6 'White 20', probably belonging to 4./JG 54 at Immola in July 1944. The aircraft features the yellow Eastern Front Theatre band around the fuselage 'under' the cross, which extend onto the rear section of the canopy hood. Note the Ju 87 'Stukas' in formation overhead. [SA-kuva]

Left hand page bottom:
Ground crew at work on II./JG 54's Fw 190A-6s at Immola in July 1944 as a formation of Ju 87Ds fly overhead. [SA-kuva]

much as before except that the 20mm MG-FF cannon were replaced by two further 20mm MG 151/20 cannon (the MG-FF could be reinstated if required). Because the outer wing MG 151s were mounted lower than the MG/FFs, larger, bulged fairings incorporating cartridge case ejection chutes were added to the wing lower surfaces. Reinforced weapon mounts were applied to the wings to allow (in lieu of the outer MG 151/20s) the carriage of two underslung weapon packs each with two MG 151/20s. Alternatively, some sub-types could accommodate one MK 108 30mm (1.18in) cannon within each outer wing section, while other sub-variants could accommodate two of the physically larger MK 103 30mm cannon mounted one beneath each outer wing section. Some A-6 variants were devoid of outer wing guns entirely. Most if not all Fw 190A-6s retained their twin MG 17 machine guns, possibly to assist pilots to hit their targets although, specifically, the Luftwaffe didn't use tracer ammunition in the MG 17

Top left:
II./JG 54 Fw 190A-6 taxis at Immola prior to taking off on an operational sortie in July 1944. The original upper surface RLM 74/75 camouflage scheme appears to have been modified, probably with 'solid' shades of green – note how the hakenkreuz (swastika) has been masked off and painted around. The underwing ejection chutes for the outer pair of cannon are visible from this low angle as are the type's near-circular mainwheel wells. [SA-kuva]

Centre and bottom left:
Two close-up views of the white spinners with black spirals carried by the Fw 190A-6s from II./JG 54 when based at Immola in July 1944. [Both SA-kuva]

Top right:
Groundcrew removing the propeller from an Fw 190A-6 of II./JG 54 at Immola in July 1944. [SA-kuva]

Centre right:
Ground crew examining a battle-damaged Fw 190A-6, still carrying its factory codes CY+CM after it managed to return to Immola, on 27th June 1944 revealing damage to both metal and linen alike. [SA-kuva]

Bottom right:
Fw 190A-6 from II/JG54 takes off from Immola on 28 June 1944 and while the image is somewhat blurred it is interesting insofar as it may have belonged to the Gruppen Stab. [SA-kuva]

Right hand page:
Ground crew refuelling Fw 190F-8, 'Black 6', of 1./Schlachtgeschwader 5 at Immola in June 1944. Conditions were evidently hot and fairly primitive as the groundcrew are using a hand pump to transfer the fuel from the drum to the aircraft. [SA-kuva]

Four views of Fw 190F-8, 'Black 10', of 1./SG 5 at Immola, June 1944.

Top:
Visible in this view is the ETC 501 centreline bomb rack and the letter 'E' under the port wing which may be the remnants of the aircraft's factory code. [SA-kuva]

Right:
An overall rear view of 'Black 10', showing the solid mainwheel hubs. The rear fuselage band appears to be the yellow Eastern Theatre band overpainted in a camouflage colour. Damage to the rudder has been repaired with red dope applied to the fabric patches. [SA-kuva]

which was instead loaded with high-explosive-incendiary or *Beobachtung Geschoss* observation rounds that exploded on impact, thus showing the pilot he was on target.

A new FuG 16ZE radio navigation system was fitted in conjunction with a FuG 10ZY. A loop aerial for radio navigation, mounted on a small 'teardrop' base was fitted under the rear fuselage, offset slightly to port, with an additional short 'whip' aerial aft of this. These aerials were fitted on all later Fw 190 variants.

Given its augmented firepower, some of the first A-6 fighters went straight to the hard pressed *Schlachtgruppen* on the Eastern Front where their cannon proved highly effective strafing ground targets.

On the Western Front as the air battles over the Reich intensified, many pilots came to consider their ETC 501 racks and auxiliary fuel tanks to be unnecessary. In late 1943, the Erla factory in Antwerp designed a simpler combined armament rack/drop tank fitting which was more streamlined than the bulky ETC 501 and could be quickly fitted or removed prior to take off, enabling missions to be flown with or without the rack or drop tank.

Much of the experience obtained during Fw 190A-5 operations was incorporated in the A-6, which was outfitted in numerous ways with various *Rüstsätz* (field modification) kits, allowing the flexibility of the sub-type to be further refitted in the field as missions demanded. According to

Fighters and Ground Attack

Left:
The fuselage sides also appear to have additional camouflage applied, especially noticeable around the fuselage cross and under the numeral. The SC 250 (Sprengbombe Cylindrisch 250) bombs in the foreground have coloured stripes on their tailcones, probably in yellow or perhaps red, to indicate the type of filling used. [SA-kuva]

Below:
Head-on view showing the mainwheel wells, lack of yellow wing tip under surfaces and what appears to be another factory code letter just to the right of the groundcrews' heads. [SA-kuva]

RLM acceptance reports and Focke-Wulf production books it would seem that about 960 Fw 190A-6s were built from July 1943 to April 1944, although some references quote the end of production in November 1943 after the completion of just 570 aircraft.

Fw 190A-7

Production of the Fw 190A-7 began in late 1943 powered by the BMW 801D-2 engine, again producing 1,677hp. Designed to specifically combat the USAAF's heavy bombers, the basic armament was upgraded to include two cowling-mounted 13mm MG 131s in lieu of the MG 17s. Because the breeches of the MG 131s were larger they had to be mounted further apart and the upper cowling in front of the cockpit was modified with bulged fairings. This left insufficient room for the three cowling toggle latches which were moved to the side panels. The rest of the armament fit stayed the same as earlier versions with two wing root and two outer wing MG 151/20E cannon.

The A-7 was also fitted with an updated

Top:
Fw 190A-7/Trop, 'White I' of an unidentified Schlacht unit, possibly SG 2, SG 4 or SKG 10, in Russia in 1943, being overflown by a schwarm of Messerschmitt Bf 110Gs. Note the dense mottle on the Focke-Wulf's fuselage sides and the yellow Eastern Front rear fuselage band.

Revi 16B gunsight replacing the older C/12D model. The additional weight of the new weapons system required strengthening of the mainwheels by adding a reinforced rim to better deal with typical frontline airfield conditions.

There were several major *Rüstsätz* for the A-7, many including the WGr 21 'stovepipe' rockets, and a special version, the A-7/R2 that carried a 30mm MK 108 cannon in the outer wing positions, the larger breech of the MK 108 cannon resulting in a rectangular fairing on top of the wing near the flap line. The first of these heavy fighters, specifically designed to combat the USAAF's four-engine heavy bombers, called *Viermöte* by Luftwaffe pilots, left the Fieseler production lines in Kassel in early 1944. First deliveries went to I./JG 11 based at Rotenburg near Hanover. In early 1944 JG 11 was one of the most successful Fw 190 fighter units facing the USAAF onslaught on the Western Front. They also suffered the heaviest losses of any *Jagdwaffe* unit in March 1944.

Other units that flew the A-7 'bomber-destroyer' were *Sturmstaffel 1*, which was integrated into IV.(Sturm)/JG 3 in late April 1944; I./JG 1 and II./JG 300. A total of 800 Fw 190A-7s were produced from November 1943 to April 1944 according to RLM acceptance reports and Focke-Wulf production books. The sub-type was replaced on the production lines by the Fw 190A-8.

Fw 190A-8
In many ways, the Fw 190A-8 was the ultimate A-series variant and numerically the most important Fw 190 fighter. More A-8s with their various bomber-destroyer *Rüstsätz* kits were built than all the other A series variants put together, which says much about the type of war the *Jagdwaffe* was now fighting.

Production of the Fw 190A-8 started in February 1944, powered either by a BMW 801D-2 or the 801Q/TU, a standard 801D with thicker armour on the front annular cowling which also incorporated the oil tank. The same basic BMW 801D-2 engine powered the A-8 as the A-3 of 1942, so various forms of short term engine power boosting was an important feature on this variant. Additional boost was necessary to compete with Allied fighters. Such changes introduced on the Fw 190A-8 included the C3-injection *Erhöhte Notleistung* emergency boost system which sprayed additional fuel into the fuel/air mix, cooling it and allowing higher boost pressures to be run raising power to 1,953hp for a short time, but at the cost of much higher fuel consumption. Externally this feature can be recognised by the small

yellow ring painted in the bottom corner of the upper cowl machine gun cover.

A new internal 118-litre (26-gallon) fuel tank mounted in the rear fuselage behind the cockpit could serve as a fuel tank or, in the /R4 variant, be replaced by a nitrous oxide tank for GM-1 power boost at higher altitudes, causing the radio equipment to be moved forward just behind the pilot. A large square hatch with rounded corners was cut into the lower fuselage to enable the new tank to be installed, and the pilot's oxygen bottles were moved aft and positioned around this hatch. A fuel filler was added to the port side below the rear canopy, and a rectangular radio access hatch was added to the starboard side.

This tank installation moved the centre of gravity backwards and, as a cure, the under-fuselage mounted rack, on a lengthened carrier, was moved 200mm

This page:
Two photos of an Fw 190A-7/R6 fitted with the air-to-air missile launcher WGr 21 'Werfgranat' or 'stove pipe', which fired time-fused shells. Still carrying its factory codes KU+BG, the aircraft and weapon system is presumably undergoing testing. The WGr 21 weapon was designed to break up American bomber 'box formations' and operational aircraft so equipped were often referred to as 'Pulk Zerstörern' (Formation Destroyers).

Above:
A busy scene showing ground crew refuelling and re-arming an Fw 190A-7 of I Gruppe JG 11, either at Rotenburg or Wunstorf, in early 1944. Note the MG 151 bulged cartridge case ejection chute panel hanging down while virtually all of the cowling panels have been opened to allow access to the engine and the fuselage MG 131s.

(7.87in) forward. This rack became standard on the A-8 model and the fuselage design would form the basis for all later variants of the Fw 190 onwards, including the 'long-nosed' Fw 190D and Ta 152 series. The A-8 was equipped with a FuG 16 ZY radio set that despite the circular radio navigation antenna, featured a Morane aerial for the *Y-Verfahren* fitted as standard under the port wing, just aft of the mainwheel well.

From the A-8 onwards, Fw 190s could be seen fitted with a new paddle-bladed propeller (the VDM 9), identified by its wide blades with curved tips. A new bulged canopy hood with greatly improved vision to the front and side – developed for the Fw 190F-2 ground-attack model – was often seen fitted on A-8s. The new canopy incorporated an increased area of head armour which was supported by reinforced bracing and a large fairing.

A useful recognition feature when endeavouring to differentiate between the A-7 and the A-8, was the repositioning of the pitot tube which shifted from the starboard leading edge mid-wing position to the wing tip. To simplify production, the bulge for the MK 108 cannon breech near the flap line also appeared on most A-8s, (and indeed most F-8s). It did not affect performance and made for a somewhat more 'universal' wing as far as production was concerned.

The Fw 190A-8, like previous Fw 190 models, could be equipped with different *Rüstsätz* kits namely: R1, R2, R3, R4, R6, R7, R8, R11 and R12, although R1, R3 and R4 were abandoned shortly after and generally it was the R6 and R7 kits that were used, plus the A-8/R2 and A-8/R8 *Sturmbock (literally 'battering ram')* models. The *Einsatzstaffel* of the little-known *Jagdgruppe 10*, a unit formed from *Erprobungskommando 25*, designated 3./JGr 10 had some A-8s equipped with the rearward firing *Krebsgerät*, with at least three featuring a red and yellow snake motif along the entire length of the fuselage, with black *Staffel* numbers outlined in red and a small *Geschwader*-type code 'IL' behind the fuselage *balkenkreuze* – something rarely seen on fighter variants of the Fw 190. Fw 190A-8s of 12.(Sturm)/JG 3 were also fitted with the *Krebsgerät* but it wasn't put into widespread use.

In its *Sturmjäger* (bomber-destroyer)

Fighters and Ground Attack

Top:
Fw 190A-7 of 1./JG 1 at Dortmund-Brackel, in Germany's North Rhine-Westphalia region in January 1944. The pilot (thought to be Hptm Alfred Grislawski, Staffelkapitän of 1 Staffel), obscures the bulged fairings associated with the fuselage-mounted 13mm MG 131s, while the long barrels of the wing-mounted 20mm MG 151 cannon are visible as is the starboard undercarriage's plain mainwheel hub with strengthened rim. Of interest is the Geschwader's 'winged 1' emblem on the cowling which was introduced by Oberstleutnant Walter Oesau, Geschwaderkommodore JG 1 in September 1943. This aircraft also features the yellow cowling underside (which looks darker due to the type of film used), armoured windscreen, Revi 16B gunsight, JG 1's broad red rear fuselage Geschwader identification band and a white spinner.

configuration the Fw 190A-8 weighed well over 5,500kg (12,125lb) the all-up weight having increased by about 2,000kg (4,441lb) over earlier versions and in this configuration the aircraft was totally unsuited for fighter-versus-fighter combat. Because of its poor high altitude performance, the *Sturmjäger* bomber-destroyers were normally escorted into action by high altitude, high performance variants of the Bf 109G. Increasingly, tactics were standardised around large battle formations comprising dedicated fighters to deal with the USAAF fighter escorts and the heavy *Sturmjäger* to attack the four-engine bombers.

Appearing in service from April/May 1944, the *Sturmjäger* Fw 190A-8/R2 variants operated by the *Sturmgruppen* were equipped with 30mm MK 108 cannon in lieu of any outer wing MG 151/20 cannon. Fw 190A-8s quickly superseded the A-7 variant on the production line. To offer some protection from the USAAF bombers' formidable defensive fire as the *Sturmjäger* closed-in from the rear, they were fitted with 30mm canopy and windscreen armoured glass. Additionally, approximately 200kg (441lb) of appliqué armour was affixed to protect both the cockpit and engine.

More often than not, these aircraft had their 13mm cowling machine guns removed and their troughs faired over to save weight and drag, in which configuration they became the /R8 *Rüstsätz*. Armament configuration of the *standard* A-8 was the same as that of the A-7, although in many cases the outboard MG 151/20 wing cannon were removed in

Left:
Fw190A-8, W/Nr 171568, a Cottbus-built machine coded 'Yellow 7' from an unidentified 6 Staffel in a somewhat 'distressed state' but still carrying a 300-litre centreline-mounted drop tank. Of interest is the fuselage balkenkreuze without the thin black outline which, together with the 'open' outline-only cross on the wing upper surfaces was introduced during 1943. The swastika lacks a thin black outline and the rudder appears to be yellow.

order to improve performance. For many *Jagdwaffe* pilots flying the Fw 190 over the homeland, this modification was the very least that was required to stand a chance in air-to-air combat against Allied fighters.

Over 6,550 A-8 airframes were manufactured from February 1944 to May 1945 and the type was produced by at least eight factories during its lifetime.

Left hand page top:
Fw 190A-8, W/Nr 175140, 'Red 6' of another unidentified Geschwader, but belonging to 5 Staffel, in a classic 'Kopfstand' (nose-over) position, possibly on the same airfield as 'Yellow 7'. Again, the fuselage cross is without a thin black outline, as too are the Balkenkreuze under the wings. An ETC 501 centreline rack is in place minus the 300-litre drop tank.

Left hand page bottom:
Line up of Fw 190A-8/R2s of 4.(Sturm)/JG 300, in late 1944. Armed with two MG 151/20 20mm and two MK 108 30mm cannon in the wings, Sturmgruppen Fw 190s were charged with breaking up the formations of USAAF daylight bombers and pilots were expected to close in to extremely short-range combat and even contemplate deliberately ramming the enemy bombers when circumstances permitted. 'White 5' (W/Nr 687366?) is in the foreground, with 'White 15 'and 'White 18' identifiable amongst the other aircraft. (Courtesy of Chris Goss)

This page:
Two views of an Fw 190A-8, W/Nr 739141, 'chevron 1' (possibly of a stabskette (staff flight)), photographed after force-landing in Denmark towards the end of the war. The national markings feature variations of late-war styles with the fuselage balkenkreuze being reduced to a black outline only with a plain black swastika. It also appears that the fuselage and fin have been overpainted, which is particularly noticeable around the swastika. (NMD)

Above:
Various Luftwaffe aircraft photographed at Kastrup, Denmark, after the German surrender in May 1945. The two Fw 190s, both A-8s, show different markings applications – 'Yellow 1' on the left (with the 'blown' canopy), has JG 301's yellow and red Geschwader identification bands and a black outline-only fuselage cross and swastika on the fin, whereas 'Black 12' (unit unknown) in the foreground has a black with white outline fuselage cross with a similar swastika. The He 219A-0 'Uhu' on the right is believed to be W/Nr 210901, B4+AA, of Nachtjadgstaffel Norwegen.
A 41 Sqn Spitfire XIV sits in the background. (NMD)

Fw 190A-9

The Fw 190A-9 was essentially the final production model of the A-series. Production started in the autumn of 1944 and continued in parallel with the A-8 variant. The A-9 was powered by the then new BMW 801S – called the 801TS or 801TH when delivered as a complete 'power egg' installation, a system embraced by the Luftwaffe for a number of engine types on operational aircraft, in part for easy field replacement. Rated at 1,973hp, monthly output of completed A-9 airframes depended on the limited deliveries of these engines. It was originally intended that the A-9 should be powered by the 2400hp BMW 801F engine, but BMW had not started production of these engines in time, consequently the 801S was substituted instead.

An important component of the new engine was the 14-blade cooling fan and a heavier 10mm (.39in) armoured ring on the front annular cowling incorporating the oil cooler tank. As such, Fw 190A-9s can be identified by this larger armoured ring, or by looking into the engine and counting the cooling-fan blades. Unfortunately, the 14-blade cooling fan required more power to operate and consequently it didn't really improve anything and so BMW reverted to the 12-blade fan.

The 'blown' canopy design incorporating the larger head armour was fitted as standard, but because it lacked an aerial-tensioning device the antenna would fall slack along the fuselage when the canopy was open. Three types of propeller were authorised for use on the A-9 – the VDM 9-12176A wooden propeller was the preferred option as it increased climb performance, however, many A-9s were fitted with the standard VDM 9-12067A metal propeller and some had a VDM 9-12153A metal propeller with external bolt-on pitch/balance weights. All three measured 3.5m (11ft 6in) in diameter.

The A-9 was very similar to the A-8 in regard to the armament and *Rüstsätz* kits that could be fitted. JG 301 received the first Fw 190A-9s off the Focke-Wulf Cottbus production line in September 1944, but by autumn, like other former *'Wilde Sau'* night fighting units, JG 301 had long since reverted to the daylight

Below:
Fw 190A-8 captured also at Kastrup, Denmark, after the German surrender in May 1945. Of note is the armoured cowling ring, additional camouflage on the wing leading edges and the 'missing' MK 108 30mm cannon in the outer position of the starboard wing. (NMD)

Right:
A member of the Danish Resistance photographed sitting in an otherwise anonymous captured Fw 190A-8 following the German surrender in May 1945. This image serves primarily to illustrate the blown canopy hood and associated 'solid' headrest frame and the prominent wing root fairing rivets. The 'Red 20' (outlined in white) appears to have been applied to a recently repainted panel. (NMD)

Below:
The remains of an Fw 190A-8, W/Nr 682989, from a batch built by Fieseler at Kassel, pictured at an airfield in the vicinity of Nuremberg, Bavaria, in 1946. The code 'White 21' would indicate a 4 Staffel machine, but the II Gruppe horizontal 'bar' which appears to be red (partially outlined with a thin white border) runs across the full width of JG 301's yellow and red Geschwader identification band indicating a 6 Staffel machine! It is known that II./JG 301 operated a mix of Fw 190 A-8s and A-9s, many of which seem to have had 'high' staffel numbers, all with red II Gruppe bars over the yellow and red Geschwader identification band, which may have been a common II Gruppe feature irrespective of the staffel. In this instance the balkenkreuze has an obvious white outline while the swastika is plain black. (NARA)

fighter role. During the autumn of 1944 it was hoped that those pilots who had been trained in blind flying techniques could form a specialist unit and as such some of JG 301's A-9s were fitted with the R11 *Rüstsätz* featuring the PKS 12 auto pilot and heated canopy glass. But losses and a lack of experienced formation leaders meant that this idea would be still-born.

Focke-Wulf 190A-9s in JG 301 service were generally equipped with two 20mm cannon and two 13mm MGs, although outer wing cannon could be mounted. A total of 910 A-9s were built between April 1944 and May 1945, mostly in Focke-Wulf's Cottbus factory.

Above:
Fw 190A-8, W/Nr 170638, 'White 11' of an unidentified unit abandoned at Berlin-Gatow, Germany, May 1945. A Focke-Wulf Cottbus-built machine, it displays circular ring-style 'mottling' on the cowling, a feature seen only on a few airframes; possibly the handiwork of a particular sub-contractor or even a paint shop individual. The aircraft has late war 'simplified' national markings consisting of black outline only crosses on the fuselage sides while the swastika has a white outline.

Left:
Close-up of the cockpit area of an Fw 190A-8 showing the bulged cowling over the 13mm machine guns and the later-style 'blown' canopy hood with revised head armour and solid rear fairing. The aircraft is thought to be W/Nr 961118, 'Red 5' of 2./JG 6 being surrendered (by an unknown pilot) at Fürth, northern Bavaria, in May 1945.

Schlachtflieger – dedicated ground attack

Above:
An abandoned Fw 190F-8 found near Berlin in 1945. By this date the aircraft would probably have been finished in one of the late-war colour combinations of either RLM 75 Mittelgrau and RLM 83 Dunkelgrün or RLM 81 Braunviolett and possibly RLM 83 Dunkelgrün upper surfaces. Of interest is the black numeral '1' outlined in white possibly suggesting that a Stab chevron might also have been applied, albeit one obscured by the wing in this image.

Dedicated ground attack variants

The **Fw 190F** series was developed from the *Umrüstbausätz* U4-equipped Fw 190As. Early testing started in May 1942 on an Fw 190A-0 test bed aircraft fitted with centreline and wing-mounted ETC 50 bomb racks. The early results were quite good and Focke-Wulf began engineering a dedicated 'attack' version of the Fw 190. Additional armour was added to the bottom of the fuselage to protect the fuel tanks, pilot, engine cowling, landing gear mechanism and outer wing mounted armament. Finally, the *Umrüstbausätz* 3 kit was fitted to the aircraft by means of an ETC 501 or ER 4 centreline mounted bomb rack with up to an SC 250 bomb under each wing. This aircraft was designated the Fw 190F-1 although the first thirty were essentially Fw 190A-4/U3s. However, Focke-Wulf continued assembling the aircraft on the production line as the **Fw 190F-1**, with eighteen more being built before switching to the F-2.

The **Fw 190F-2** was the Fw 190A-5/U3 renamed, which were assembled as Fw 190F-2s on the production line. Some 270 Fw 190F-2s were built according to Focke-Wulf production logs and RLM acceptance reports.

The **Fw 190F-3** was based upon the Fw 190A-5/U17, which was fitted with a centreline mounted ETC 501 bomb rack, and in the Fw 190F-3/R1 and Fw 190F-3/R-3 sub-types, two double ETC 50 bomb racks could be fitted under each wing or, alternatively, two similarly located 30mm MK 103 cannon. The F-3 could carry a 300-litre drop tank. A total of 432 Fw 190F-3s were built.

Due to difficulties creating an Fw 190F sub-type able to effectively strafe Russian T-34 tanks, the **F-4 to F-7** models were abandoned, and all attempts were focused on conversions of the Fw 190A-8 into the F-8.

The **Fw 190F-8** differed from the standard A-8 by having a slightly modified injector on the compressor which increased performance for several minutes at lower altitudes. The F-8 was also fitted with the improved FuG 16 ZS radio unit which provided much better communication with ground combat units. Armament on the Fw 190F-8 comprised two 20mm MG 151/20 cannon in the wing roots and two 13mm MG 131 machine guns above the engine. According to RLM acceptance reports, at least 3,400 F-8s were built up to December 1944, and probably several hundred more

from February to May 1945. Data covering these months is missing and presumed to be irretrievably lost. Dozens of F-8s served as test beds for anti-tank armament including the WGr 28 280mm (11in) air-to-ground missile, the 88mm (3.46in) *Panzerschreck 2* rockets, *Panzerblitz 1* and R4M rockets.

There were also several *Umrüstbausätz* kits developed for the F-8, which included the Fw 190F-8/U1 long range *Jabo* with underwing V.Mtt Schloss shackles to hold two 300-litre fuel tanks. ETC 503 bomb racks were also fitted, allowing the Fw 190F-8/U1 to carry one SC 250 bomb under each wing and an SC 250 bomb on the centreline.

The Fw 190F-8/U2 torpedo bomber was fitted with an ETC 503 bomb rack under each wing and a centreline mounted ETC 504. The /U2 was also equipped with the TSA 2 A weapons sighting system that improved the /U2's ability to attack seaborne targets with a 700kg (1,543lb) BT 700 torpedo. The Fw 190F-8/U3 heavy torpedo bomber was fitted with an ETC 502, which allowed it to carry one 1400kg (3,086lb) BT-1400 heavy torpedo. Due to

Above:
Fw 190F-8/R1 ground attack fighters possibly of II./SG 10, based in Hungary in early 1945. At least two of the aircraft (first and third in line) appear to have the yellow nose band introduced in March 1945 for aircraft operated by Luftflotte 4. In addition to any other markings carried, Luftwaffe aircraft operating in Hungary were generally identified by a yellow 'V' applied beneath the port wing. The aircraft seen here have had bomb racks fitted beneath their outer wings.

Left:
An Fw 190F-8/R1, probably from SG 2 based in Hungary during the winter of 1944/45, in a well-worn and patchy 'winter white' temporary camouflage scheme. The lower mainwheel leg covers have been removed – a regular occurrence to avoid compacted snow affecting the brakes.

Above:
An abandoned Fw 190F-8, found at Pardubice, Czechoslovakia, that was previously operated by SG 77. Fitted with ETC 71 outer wing bomb racks as well as the centreline ETC 501 rack, the upper surfaces are believed to be in the late-war two-tone green RLM 82 Hellgrün and RLM 83 Dunkelgrün combination. Note the white spinner with a black spiral.

Right:
Close-up of a Hungarian Air Force (Magyar Királyi Honvéd Légierő – MKHL) Fw 190F-8. Approximately seventy-two Fw 190F-8s were delivered to the MKHL from November 1944 and were operated by the 102 Vadászbombázó Század (102nd Fighter-Bomber Squadron, later 102 Fighter Bomber Wing), engaged in close-support missions on the Eastern Front. 'White 54' is armed with a centreline-mounted SC 250 bomb and four 'sharkmouthed' wing-mounted SC 50 bombs. For low-altitude attacks, bombs such as the SC 50 could be fitted with an extended striker or Stachelbombe (Spike Bomb – or simply Stabo) causing them to explode above ground level as opposed to in it. 102 Vadászbombázó Század successfully operated the Fw 190F until the final days of the war with many being named as indeed was 'MICA' applied in this instance on the machine gun cowling. (Fortepan-Zsuzsa Vargha via HMP)

Schlachtflieger - dedicated ground attack

Above:
With lower mainwheel leg covers removed and equipped with a blown canopy, this Fw 190F-8 displays the distinctive 'stripey' temporary white snow camouflage as applied by SG 2 in Hungary in early 1945. Both aircraft seen here are carrying AB 250 munitions containers on their centreline ETC 501 racks.

Left:
MG 131 equipped Fw 190F-8 belonging to I./SG 4 being dug out of a hole. I./SG 4 operated in Italy in the ground attack role until July 1944 when the Gruppe was transferred to the Eastern Front. The aircraft is finished in a hastily applied Mediterranean Theatre camouflage scheme of RLM 79 Sandgelb with RLM 80 Olivgrün mottling, which had been painted over its original factory-applied RLM 74/75 upper surface 'greys' scheme. Note I./SG 4's axe-wielding Mickey Mouse riding a bomb on the cowling and the undercarriage up/down indicator on the wing's upper surface.

Above:
A rotte of Fw 190Gs over Romania, possibly of II./SG 2 or II./SG 4. The Fw 190G, built as a long-range attack aircraft – Jagdbomber mit vergrösserter Reichweite, or Jabo Rei – followed the success of the Fw 190F as a close support aircraft and was used right up to the end of hostilities.

Below:
A pair of ground attack Fw 190s, possibly F-3s, of an unidentified Schlacht unit in Russia during the winter of 1943-44. Both are fitted with tropical air filters and are armed with SC 250 bombs on their ETC 501 centreline racks ready for their next sortie. The fuselage balkenkreuze on the farthest aircraft appears to have had the white areas painted out using the under surface colour. The two bombs visible have both been painted in different colours with the one under the nearest aircraft being dark (perhaps RLM 71) while the other is light, possibly RLM 65.

Schlachtflieger - dedicated ground attack

the size of the torpedo, the /U3's tailwheel leg needed to be lengthened. The /U3 was fitted with a 2,000hp PS BMW 801S engine and a Ta 152-style fin, rudder and tail unit.

The Fw 190F-8/U4 night fighter was equipped with exhaust manifold flame dampers and various electrical systems such as the FuG 101 radio altimeter, PKS 12 automatic pilot and the TSA 2 A sighting system. Weapons fitted ranged from torpedoes to bombs, however, the /U4 was only armed with two MG 151/20 cannon as a fixed armament.

The Fw 190F-9 was based on the Fw 190A-9 but received a Ta 152 tail unit, a bulged canopy as fitted to late-build A-9s, and four ETC 50 or ETC 70 bomb racks under the wings. According to RLM acceptance reports approximately 147 F-9s were built in January 1945, and perhaps several hundred more from February to May 1945. Again, data for these months appears to be missing and is probably lost.

Fw 190G

The Fw 190G was built as a long-range attack aircraft, *Jagdbomber mit vergrösserter Reichweite* or *Jabo Rei*. Following the success of the Fw 190F as a close support aircraft, both the Luftwaffe and Focke-Wulf began investigating ways of extending the range of the Fw 190F and from these tests, the Fw 190G was born. There were four distinct versions of the Fw 190G.

The **Fw 190G-1** was the first, based upon the Fw 190A-4/U8. Initial testing found that if all but two wing root mounted 20mm MG 151 cannon (with a reduced ammunition load) were removed, the sub-type could carry a 250kg or 500kg bomb on the centreline and up to a 250kg bomb under each wing. Typically, the Fw 190G-1 flew with underwing fuel tanks, fitted on VTr Ju 87 racks. The FuG 25a IFF (identification friend/foe) was fitted on occasion as well as one of the various radio direction finders available at the time. With the removal of the fuselage mounted MG 17s, an additional oil tank was fitted to support the BMW 801D-2 engine's longer run times.

The **Fw 190G-2** was based on the Fw 190A-5/U8 and was similarly equipped to the G-1; however, due to wartime conditions, the underwing drop tank racks were replaced with the much simpler V.Mtt Schloss fittings which allowed for a number of underwing configurations. Some G-2s were also fitted with the additional oil tank in place of the MG 17s while other G-2s were fitted with exhaust dampers as well as landing lights in the leading edge of the port wing for night operations.

The **Fw 190G-3** was based on Fw 190A-6 and like the earlier G models, all but the two wing root mounted MG 151 cannon were removed. The new V.Fw Trg bomb racks allowed the G-3 to simultaneously carry fuel tanks and bomb loads. Because of the enhanced range bestowed upon it by the two additional fuel tanks, the G-3's duration increased to two hours thirty minutes. Due to this extra flight duration, a PKS 11 autopilot was fitted. Some G-3s built in late 1943 were

Above:
Two Fw 190G-3s thought to be of II./SchG 1, probably photographed during Operation 'Citadel', the huge tank battle around Kursk in July 1943. Ground attack units tended to use letters rather than numerals for aircraft identification – the white letter and II Gruppe horizontal bar almost certainly identifying them as 4 Staffel machines. The aircraft would have been finished in the mid-war 'greys' scheme and have the lower mainwheel leg covers removed.

Above:
An Fw 190F-8, (possibly W/Nr 588717) of the Gruppe Stab II./SG 77. Examination of the photo reveals a large numeral '3', probably in Stab green, immediately in front of the fuselage balkenkreuze and just to the rear of the black and white chevron. The national markings are a mix of mid-war black with white outline crosses and late-war black outline only swastika. Unfortunately, this aircraft's camouflage scheme is hard to determine, our presumption being that it might be one of the late-war combinations.

also fitted with the modified BMW 801D-2 engine which allowed for increased low-altitude performance for short periods. The G-3 had two primary *Rüstsätz* kits, the /R1 which replaced the V.Fw. Trg racks with WB 151/20 cannon pods, giving the G-3/R1 a total of six 20mm cannon. When fitted with the /R1 kit, the G model's addition armour was typically not fitted and the PKS 11 autopilot was removed. The G-3/R1 was used in both ground attack and anti-bomber roles. The /R5 was similar to the /R1, but the V.Fw Trg racks were removed and two ETC 50 racks per wing added. As with the /R1, the additional armour from the basic G model was removed, as was the additional oil tank. In some instances, cowl-mounted MG 17s were refitted.

The **Fw 190G-8** was based on the Fw 190A-8, used the same 'blown' canopy as the F-8 and was fitted with underwing ETC 503 racks that could carry either bombs or drop tanks. Two primary *Rüstsätz* kits were planned for the F-8. The /R4 was a refit for the GM 1 engine boost system, but never made it into production, but the /R5 kit replaced the ETC 503 racks with two ETC 50 or 71 racks. Due to the similarities with the F-8, the G-8 was only in production for a short time, however, some Gs were field-modified to carry 1,000kg (2,204lb), 1,600kg (3527lb) and 1,800kg (3968lb) bombs fitted with improved main landing gear with enhanced oleo struts and reinforced tyres.

Approximately 1,300 Fw 190Gs of all variants were built as new. Due to wartime conditions, the manufacturing environment and the use of special workshops, the actual number of G models built is almost impossible to determine. During the later war years, 'composite' aircraft were often assembled. For example, the wings from a fuselage-damaged aircraft and the fuselage from a wing-damaged aircraft might be re-assembled into a new aircraft and listed as a Fw 190G with a new *werknummer*.

Below:
RAF personnel looking over an Fw 190A-8 at Lüneburg airfield in May 1945. Still carrying a 300-litre centreline fuel tank, the aircraft appears to be fitted with broad VDM 9 (either metal or wooden) propeller blades and a blown canopy hood although the associated 'solid' head rest frame is missing. Thought to be coded 'Yellow 5' with a faded yellow horizontal II Gruppe bar, it also has what appears to be a narrow red Reichsverteidigung (Defence of the Reich) Geschwader identification band on the rear fuselage, possibly indicating an aircraft from 6./JG 300. Narrow red rear fuselage bands were used by the unit on its Wilde Sau night fighters, which were later widened for day fighter use, although JG 300 adopted blue/white/blue Geschwader identification bands in December 1944 to avoid confusion with JG 1 which also used red bands. (HMP)

Mistel and Trainers

Above:
A complete Mistel composite as photographed at Merseburg airfield, near Leipzig, Germany following its capture by troops of the US 1st Army in April 1945. The lower component is a Junkers Ju 88G-1, W/Nr 590153, with additional camouflage applied to its original night fighter scheme of overall RLM 76 Lichtblau with RLM 75 Mittelgrau mottling, in the so-called westenmüller – mirror-wave/meander/scribble – pattern (possibly using greens and greys) that was applied to the upper surfaces of the main and tailplanes, fuselage spine and fin and rudder in the field. The controlling Fw 190F-8 also features what appear to be areas of 'locally' applied overpainting in addition to the number '97' applied to its rudder. Note the many variations of national markings shown in this image. (NARA)

Centre right:
Focke-Wulf Fw 190S-8, W/Nr 931327, 'Yellow 50' from an unidentified Jagdfliegerschule found abandoned in Germany in May 1945. Converted from standard single-seat airframes, often using damaged aircraft from frontline units, the rear fuselage was modified by closing off the rear portion with sheet metal and building up the fuselage sides with a duralumin superstructure. The original single-seat sliding canopy hood was replaced with a new three part, rectangular side-opening canopy. Perhaps fifty 'old' Fw 190A-5s and A-8s were converted by replacing the MW 50 tank (not required in a trainer) with a second cockpit. Originally designated Fw 190A-5/U1 and Fw 190A-8/U1, the converted two-seat airframes were later given Fw 190S-5 and Fw 190S-8 designations (S for Schulflugzeug). This example is thought to have been based on a re-cycled Fw 190F-8 and may have been finished with a solid RLM 83 Dunkelgrün fuselage spine, possibly with RLM 75 Mittelgrau and RLM 83 Dunkelgrün wings.

Bottom right:
Captured by British troops in 1945, here US troops examine a captured Mistel combination at either Tirstrup in Denmark or Bernburg, Germany (sources conflict), at the end of the war in Europe. In this instance, the Ju 88 is a G-6 variant powered by 1,726hp Junkers Jumo 213A engines whereas the previous photos show Ju 88G-1s powered by 1,667hp BMW 801 radial engines – note their different cowlings. The Fw 190A-8 control aircraft (W/Nr 733682) is currently on display at the RAF Museum at Cosford, Shropshire, and still retains the Kugelverschraubung mit Sprengbolzen fittings, the ball joints with explosive bolts, that attached it to the Mistel. (NARA)

Mistel and Trainers

Left:
Developed as a method of delivering a large quantity of explosives in one load, the Beethoven-Gerät (Beethoven Device) comprised a piloted single-engined fighter control aircraft mounted above a modified Ju 88 explosives-carrying drone, termed Mistel (Mistletoe), the composite unit was often referred to as Vater und Sohn (Father and Son) after a popular German newspaper cartoon strip. In this photo a number of 'Mistel' composites, display varying degrees of damage, can be seen on Bernburg airfield in Saxony, Germany, after an attack by the US Eighth Air Force. Only the middle example still has its control aircraft – an Fw 190A-8 (or F-8) – in place. (NARA)

Centre left:
This view reveals the starboard side of the same Mistel combination and provides additional details such as the overpainted white outlined swastika on the Ju 88's fin, and solid colour rudder trim tab. This Ju 88 has a standard nose and cockpit which were retained for ferrying and training purposes that was later removed and the entire nose section replaced by a shaped charge with a specialised 1,800kg (3,960lb) warhead with either a copper or aluminium liner. The warhead was expected to penetrate up to seven metres of reinforced concrete. (NARA)

Bottom left:
Despite being a post-war photo taken at an air display, probably RAF Chivenor, Devon in 1973, this is a genuine Fw 190S-8 (aka Fw 190F-8/U1/) two-seat trainer, W/Nr 584219, that was captured at Grove airfield, Denmark, in May 1945. With the repurposing of dive bomber units into fighter-bomber units, the Luftwaffe began to phase out the Ju 87 and replace it with the Fw 190, creating a need to convert Ju 87 pilots to the Fw 190 as quickly as possible. Hence the requirement for a Schulflugzeug (literally 'school aircraft') variant of the Fw 190. Originally coded `Black 38', this Fw 190S-8 is thought to have been attached to Jagdfliegerschule 103 and used as a conversion trainer and a high-speed liaison aircraft. Built in early 1944, by Arado at Warnemünde as a standard Fw 190F-8, at some point in 1944, W/Nr 584219 was converted to two-seat standard by R Sochor Fabrik at Blanz-Blansko in Poland. Surrendered at Grove airfield, Denmark, in May 1945, 'Black 38' was flown back to the UK and stored at several RAF bases until being restored at St Athan in the 1970s and 80s, before being delivered to the RAF Museum Hendon in 1989, where it remains on display today, painted in the markings of I./JG 54.

The Fw 190 in captivity

Riight:
Close-up of the tropical filter fitted to the BMW-engined sub-types, which can be compared with the standard enclosed fairing of the Fw 190A-5 on the opposite page (p78). In this instance the Fw 190A-5/Trop was captured in Tunisia by the 85th Fighter Squadron 'Flying Skulls', 79th Fighter Group, USAAF, of which there are more photos of the aircraft on pages 80 and 81.

Below left and below:
A captured Focke-Wulf Fw 190A-5 being tested by the US Navy's Naval Air Test Center, Patuxent River, Maryland, circa March 1944. The aircraft, W/Nr 6005, received standard US star and bar markings and was reportedly repainted in the then standard US Navy three-tone camouflage scheme of Non Specular Sea Blue and Intermediate Blue upper surfaces with Insignia White under surfaces. The division of the two upper surface colours can just be discerned in the curved demarcation on the fuselage sides. As with most captured aircraft on test duties, all the armament was removed. (USNHHC)

Top left:
Fw 190A-8, W/Nr 681497, once coded 'White 11' of 4./JG 4, force landed at St Trond airfield (A-92), Belgium, on 1st January 1945 during Operation 'Bodenplatte'. The pilot Gefreiter Walter Wagner made a dead-stick landing causing only minor damage, following which groundcrew of the resident P-47 equipped 404th Fighter Group, 9th US Air Force, were able to repair it with parts from a nearby Luftwaffe storage area. All guns were removed and the gun ports faired over. Overpainted in bright red with the wing roots and area aft of the exhaust manifolds painted black, the aircraft had USAAF star and bar national insignia applied in the standard positions above the port and below the starboard wings and either side of the fuselage. Allocated the code 'OO-L', ('L-OO' on the starboard side and 'OO-L' on the port); a serial number of sorts (1-1-45) was also applied in black on either side of the fin and is believed to be a reference to the date it was forced down. 'OO-L' retained 4./JG 4's Knight's Helmet in a shield on the port side of the cowling. The aircraft underwent engine tests and taxiing trials and despite official permission never being granted to fly it, the 404th FG's commanding officer, Lt.Col Leo C Moon, planned a test flight with a P-47 escort but due to worries about the undercarriage it was never flown again. (NARA)

These two pages: Focke-Wulf Fw 190A-5/Trop, captured by the 85th Fighter Squadron 'Flying Skulls' 79th Fighter Group, USAAF, based at Gerbini, Sicily in August 1943. (Readers are referred to the detailed caption in the colour illustration section.)

Above:
Technician Fourth Grade Leroy M Heinz, of the US 3rd Armoured Division runs up the engine of an Fw 190G near Kothen, Germany, after the airfield was captured by the US 1st Army in May 1945. (NARA)

Left:
US troops inspect an Fw 190A-8 that lies among the ruins of the Focke-Wulf Oschersleben factory, in May 1945. (NARA)

Below:
US Army Quartermaster personnel inspecting a number of Fw 190s abandoned in various states of construction at the Focke-Wulf factory at Oschersleben, Germany in 1945. (NARA)

The Fw 190 in captivity

Above:
USAAF personnel of the 354th Fighter Group inspecting captured German aircraft of No.1426 (Enemy Aircraft) Flight RAF at Boxted, Essex in April 1944. The aircraft seen include Fw 190A-5, PN999, in the forefront with Messerschmitt Bf 109G-6, VX101, and Junkers Ju 88A-6, HM509, behind. No.1426 Flight was initially formed in November 1941 at RAF Duxford with a small complement of pilots who, previously, had been maintenance test pilots whose role now was to demonstrate captured aircraft types to RAF and Allied personnel. Initially flying aircraft forced down in the Battle of Britain, the aircraft in the unit grew as later types came into RAF hands including many that had been captured overseas by the Allies and others as a result of forced landings and defections in the UK. Repainted in RAF camouflage and markings and given RAF serials, the 'Rafwaffe' moved to RAF Collyweston, Northamptonshire, in March 1943, and in early 1944 toured various USAAF bases in Britain. (NARA)

Below:
Fw 190A-5/U8, PN999, as seen while serving with No.1426 (Enemy Aircraft) Flight. Formerly W/Nr 152596 'White 6' of I./SKG 10, it was flown by Uffz Werner Ohne who became disorientated while flying a night intruder mission against southern England and landed by mistake at Manston, Kent, on 20 June 1943. After spending time at the Royal Aircraft Establishment at Farnborough and undergoing tests at the Aeroplane and Armament Experimental Establishment, Boscombe Down, Wiltshire, it was allocated No.1426 Flight on 29 June 1943. PN999 was eventually passed to 47 Maintenance Unit at Sealand for storage in November 1945. The Bf 109G-6, (VX101) was originally W/Nr 15270, 'Yellow 14' of 6./JG 53, captured at Comiso, Italy in 1943, and the Ju 88A-6 (HM509) was from 2./KuFlGr 106, which landed by mistake at RAF Chivenor on 26 November 1941. (NARA)

Bottom:
Fw 190F-8, W/Nr 933849, which was found abandoned on a Luftwaffe airfield and appropriated by W/Cdr James Francis 'Stocky' Edwards, RCAF, 127 Wing, in late 1944/early 1945. The story goes that W/Cdr Edwards spotted the Fw 190 in an adjacent field while returning from a sortie during the Allied advance through Belgium and the Netherlands and had it transported to the base where the Wing was operating from which, according to the photo's original caption was Soltau, Germany, but may possibly have been B.58 Melsbroek or B.56 Evere in Belgium. All the aircraft's Luftwaffe markings were overpainted and RAF roundels and fin flashes applied, as were the Wing Commander's initials 'JFE'. Apparently, the aircraft was unofficially flown several times, although its ultimate fate is uncertain. The Messerschmitt Bf 108 in the background also carries RAF markings and the initials 'PST' of fellow Canadian, Group Captain Percival Stanley 'Stan' Turner, who oversaw the conversion of 127 Wing on to ground attack duties and flew with the Wing on several missions. (Courtesy of Carl Vincent)

'Langnausen' development

Above:
Although not covered in this volume, it might interest readers to compare the Jumo 213-engined development of the Fw 190, the Fw 190D 'Langnasen' (long nose) to the 'short-nosed' BMW radial engined versions. Developed during spring and summer 1944, initially to improve the Fw 190's high-altitude performance against USAAF heavy bombers, it is ironic to record that the D series were rarely used against them as the changing circumstances of the war, by late 1944, meant that fighter-versus-fighter combat and ground attack missions took priority. This particular aircraft W/Nr 0055, GH+KT, powered by a liquid-cooled Jumo 213E engine with GM-1 engine boost system and driving a broad VS 9 propeller, was the V30/U1 prototype for the next generation of Fw 190 fighters, the Focke-Wulf Ta 152.*

(*Following the RLM's decision in 1944 that new fighter aircraft designations should have the name of the chief designer, therefore taking the prefix 'Ta' from Kurt Tank's surname.]

Below:
Development of the D variant continued despite planning for the Ta 152, and this particular machine is the second Fw 190D-11 prototype, V56, W/Nr 170924, which was later given the stammkennzeichen GV+CW. In order to fit the new 12-cylinder inverted-V, liquid-cooled Jumo 213 engine in to the 'Langnasen' series, both the nose and rear fuselage were extended, adding nearly 1.52m (5ft) to the fuselage length. When later fitted with a new Jumo 2134F engine, GV+CW suffered from a series of engine failures which severely delayed the D-11's entry in to Luftwaffe service.

Above:
US Army Brigadier General George C McDonald pictured beside the tail of an Fw 190D-9, W/Nr 600150 of Stab/JG 4, that was captured near Frankfurt-Main, Germany in March 1945. The Fw 190D's rear fuselage required a 50cm (19.6in) extension section, added just forward of the tail assembly's rear angled joint which gave the rear fuselage a 'stretched' appearance. This area proved the ideal canvas for the Reichsverteidigung (Defence of the Reich) Geschwader identification band as illustrated by this 'Dora' whose JG 4 black-white-black Geschwader identification band can be seen behind the Brigadier General. (NARA)

Below:
Comparison views of the Fw 190D-9's inline Jumo 213 engined cowling and the Fw 190A'-8s BMW 801 radial engine.

Fw 190 gun installations

Above:
Sufficient remains of this severely damaged Fw 190 to clearly distinguish the bulged panels covering the breeches of the twin 13mm MG 131 heavy machine guns mounted on the upper engine cowling. Additionally, while one of this airframe's inboard 20mm MG 151/20 cannon is also visible there appears to be no evidence of weapons having been mounted in the outer wing positions. This particular aircraft coded 'Yellow 10', faintly visible on the fuselage in front of the balkenkreuz, is from an unidentified unit that may have been finished in the late war 'greens' upper surface scheme of RLM 81 Braunviolett and RLM 83 Dunkelgrün indicating a late production machine. Note the simplified 'outline only' wing and fuselage balkenkreuze, (black on the fuselage and white on the wings), 'solid' black swastika on the fin and what appears to be a spanwise camouflage demarcation line on the starboard wing, separating the two camouflage colours mid chord.

MG 17
While rifle calibre machine guns had their part to play in fighter-versus-fighter combat and were retained by such stalwarts as the Fw 109, Bf 109 and Spitfire until the end of WWII, against well-armoured bombers the MG 17 was almost an irrelevance, its contribution insignificant. While there was always a chance that the 7.9mm bullets might hit softer targets, the best argument in favour of its retention lay in its use of *Beobachtung Geschoss* observation rounds in lieu of tracer ammunition – a high-explosive-incendiary round, *B-Geschoss* exploded on impact to show the pilot he was on target. Fitted with twin synchronised MG 17s in the upper engine cowling as standard from the Fw 190A-2 to the A-6, they were supplied with a thousand rounds of (mixed) ammunition per gun (rpg).
MG 17: basic data. *Calibre = 7.9mm (.31in); Weight = 12.6kg (27.7lb); Cyclic rate (non-synchronised) = 1,050 rounds per minute (rpm) approx. Length overall (oa) 1,210mm (47.6in)*

MG 131
Intended to replace the MG 17 in bombers and fighters, this compact short-recoil heavy machine gun only brought with it a marginal increase in firepower as a consequence of having to use a small cartridge of modest power to enable the gun to fit into the limited space available. A pair of synchronised MG 131s were mounted on most, but not all, Fw 190s from the A-7 onwards supplied with 400 rpg.
MG 131: basic data. *Calibre = 13mm (.51in); Weight = 17kg (37.4lb); Cyclic rate (non-synchronised) = 900 rpm; Length (oa) 1,170mm (46in)*

MG-FF
Excluding initial prototypes and early development examples, most Fw 190s were armed with two or four 20mm cannon and two rifle-calibre machine guns. The 20mm MG-FF (developed from the Swiss FF F) was a low-velocity weapon with a relatively slow rate of fire which was adopted by the Luftwaffe in the 1930s due to its relatively light and compact design, and because its inclusion in the Fw 190's outer wing section didn't impinge greatly on the fighter's agility. Accepted at a time when most European air forces relied primarily upon rifle-calibre machine guns, the MG-FF provided a considerable increase in destructive power in a close-range fighter-to-fighter contest where its low muzzle velocity and trajectory drop was of no great issue. It was effective against bombers too, albeit, compared to later high-velocity weapons the MG-FF's limitations obliged fighter pilots to close with their targets thus denying them the option of sitting beyond the effective range of a bomber's power-operated turrets.

From the Fw 190A-2 to the A-5 series, provision was made for the installation of one MG-FF cannon in

Left:
This photo provides a clear view of the MG-FF's muzzle as well as the wing root-mounted 20mm MG 151/20E cannon and the barrels of both cowling-mounted 7.92mm MG 17s. Shorter than the MG 151 by 440mm, the MG-FF (developed from the Swiss FF F) was a low-velocity weapon with a relatively slow rate of fire and was adopted by the Luftwaffe in the 1930s because of its relatively light weight and compact design. If carried at all, then one such cannon was fitted in each outer-wing station as shown here. This image also illustrates the tightly cowled, 14-cylinder, two-row BMW 801 radial engine which powered the early Fw 190As and reveals the neatly grouped (port side) exhaust manifolds.

each outer wing panel although in practice they were frequently not installed at all, but when they were it gave pilots three types of gun – each with different ballistic properties – which rather calls into question the usefulness of the MG 17 as a sighting weapon for the MG-FF!

Each MG-FF was fed from a drum magazine containing sixty rounds; however, some sources quote fifty-five rpg. One wonders if the discrepancy reflects, perhaps, a need to avoid overstressing the feed mechanism and consequent jamming by slightly reducing the number of rounds carried. Such a possibility is not without precedent.

MG-FF: basic data. *Calibre = 20mm (.78in); Weight = 26kg approx. (57.3lb); Cyclic rate = 520 rpm; Length (oa) 1,340mm (52.7in)*

MG 151/20

Focke-Wulf production from the Fw 190A-2 saw the introduction of a pair of high-velocity MG 151/20 cannon (developed from the earlier 15mm MG 151). Mounted one in each wing root, the Fw 190 received the electrically primed 151E variant which remained standard on Fw 190s for the remainder of the war. Of necessity, the wing root mounted weapons were synchronised thus reducing their rate of fire. From the A-6 an additional pair of MG 151/20s were often mounted in lieu of the MG-FF giving the Fw 190 much greater firepower. Belt fed, the outer pair were provided with 125 rpg and the inner synchronised pair with 200 rpg. (**Note.** Sources conflict regarding the number of rounds provided for the inner pair – some state 250 rpg.)

MG 151/20: basic data. *Calibre = 20mm (.78in); Weight = 42kg (92.5lb); Cyclic rate outer pair = 700 rpm, inner (synchronised) pair 650 rpm; Length (oa) 1,770mm (69.6in)*

MK 103 (i)

Developed from the earlier MK 101, the 30mm MK 103 cannon entered service in 1943 and was intended from the outset for use against heavy bombers and armoured vehicles – albeit using the appropriate ammunition. It seems that the Fw 190 never used the MK 103 in air-to-air combat due to its weight, powerful recoil and consequent wing flexing. Several types of heavy fighter such as the He 219, Me 410, and Ju 188, among others, did make good use of the MK 103 in the bomber-destroyer role.

MK 103 (ii)

Despite early reliability issues, the MK 103 itself became a useful weapon in the anti-tank role when fitted to

Below:
For anything other than a head-on attack, it was estimated that it took an average twenty or more 20mm rounds to down a B-17 when, typically, Luftwaffe pilots were averaging half that number or less. A possible solution was to increase the number of 20mm cannon by fifty per cent from four to six. Consequently, externally mounted weapon packs were developed each containing two MG 151/20 cannon with one pack installed beneath each outer wing, necessitating the deletion of the 'standard' outer pair of wing-mounted MG 151s. This image shows Fw 190A-6/R1 prototype, W/Nr 150813, BH+CC which, following its conversion from an Fw 190A-5, was specially created for use against USAAF heavy bomber formations. The R1 was one of the few armament Rüstsätz to actually reach operational status and was available from the Fw 190A-6 onwards. BH+CC retains its inboard undercarriage doors and reveals the last three numerals of its werknummer on the cowling.

Above:
Close-up of the port wing of an Fw 190A-6/R1 fitted with the WB 151/20 weapons fairing containing a pair of 20mm MG 151/20 cannon. Loaded with 130 rpg, the gondolas increased the aircraft's weight by 380kg (838lbs). Aircraft so equipped were referred to as Pulkzerstörer (formation destroyer) and the first examples were allocated to 3./JG 11 at the end of November 1943. (Courtesy of Chris Goss)

Top right:
This image shows Fw 190A-6/R3 prototype, W/Nr 1303, RG+ZA, which was fitted with a 30mm MK 103 cannon beneath each wing; however, it was an installation that did not suit the Fw 190. Teething problems aside, there was little inherently wrong with the MK 103 which was a far larger and longer-ranging weapon than the MK 108, being successfully operated in the air-to-air role by larger and heavier aircraft than the Fw 190. Equally, the weapon proved effective (given appropriate ammunition) in the air-to-ground and anti-tank roles also. This particular aircraft and armament was tested at the Erprobungsstellen (experimental station) at Tarnewitz and was eventually allocated to I./SG 151 at Oels, Silesia, before suffering damage on 22nd January 1945. (Chris Goss)

Above:
Another example of a pod-mounted MK 103, albeit the one seen here is obviously different from the previous image inasmuch the gun barrel has been 'sheathed'. It is known that the marriage of two MK 103 with the Fw 190 airframe was compromised by vibration and wing flexing issues caused by the MK 103's weight and powerful recoil, a problem overcome in heavier aircraft where the weapon's breech and lengthy barrel could be rigidly attached to the airframe. Because the initial MK 103/R3 fairing suffered from vibration problems, a new aerodynamic front section was designed and applied as seen here, it being intended for use with the Fw 190F-8/R3 and F-9/R3; however, the entire installation was later abandoned in favour of anti-tank rockets. (Chris Goss)

dedicated ground attack aircraft such as the twin-engined Henschel Hs 129 B-2/R3 which carried a single MK 103 *rigidly* attached to the lower fuselage and supplied with 100 rounds of ammunition. Initially the gun did prove to be somewhat unreliable but when it worked as intended its hard-hitting armour-piercing projectiles (developed for use with the earlier MK 101) could penetrate armoured vehicles if they struck the sides or topsides where the armour was thinnest and depending upon the type of projectile used. Specifically, the most effective ammunition was the tungsten cored *Hartkernmunition* armour-piercing round weighing 352gm (12.4oz).

While several Fw 190 fighter-bombers existed, and had done so for some time, the pairing of the type with the MK 103 for use in the anti-tank/ground attack role appears to have begun in mid-1943 using a Fw 190A-5/R11. Two cannon were fitted but, due to their physical size, they would not fit within the wing structure itself and hence were 'underslung' – one beneath each outer wing section using *Flächengondelbewaffnung* FGB103 pods containing up to thirty-two rpg. Reportedly the pods were unsuccessful due to their weight, high recoil forces, and a degree of wing flexing which combined to reduce accuracy. Further, as tungsten became increasingly difficult to obtain in quantity, such as was available for ammunition production was reserved for infantry anti-tank weapons and for the effective 37mm cannon carried by the Ju 87G. Inevitably therefore the lack of *Hartkernmunition* reduced the pod's effectiveness still further and eventually the installation was deemed unsuccessful and didn't see a lot of use.

MK 103: basic data. *Calibre = 30mm (1.18in); Weight = 141kg (311lb); Cyclic rate = 360 rpm +; Length (oa) 2,350mm (92.5in)*

While the MG-17's relative impotence has already been referred to, it is worth mentioning that by 1943 the Luftwaffe had found even their 20mm weapons to be wanting. They discovered it took, on average, at least twenty 20mm rounds to bring down a B-17 in a stern attack, but perhaps just five or six if an accurate head-on attack could be accomplished. However, such attacks only allowed a mere half-second firing time if a collision was to be avoided – a tactic strictly for the experten.

The expenditure of a meagre twenty rounds to bring down a four-engined well-armoured bomber sounds very economical, especially considering that many Fw 190s by this time carried four MG 151/20s with c 550 rounds of ammunition, sufficient, theoretically, to bring down more than twenty-five B-17s! Fortunately for the Allies, the average Luftwaffe fighter pilot was able to hit a target maybe two per cent of the time or less – probably no better or worse than an average Allied fighter pilot – suggesting at best that ten or fewer projectiles were likely to hit the bomber. Little wonder the Luftwaffe sought more destructive weapons for its fighters at a time when USAAF B-17s, B-24s and B-26s were making incremental improvements to their frontal armour and armament.

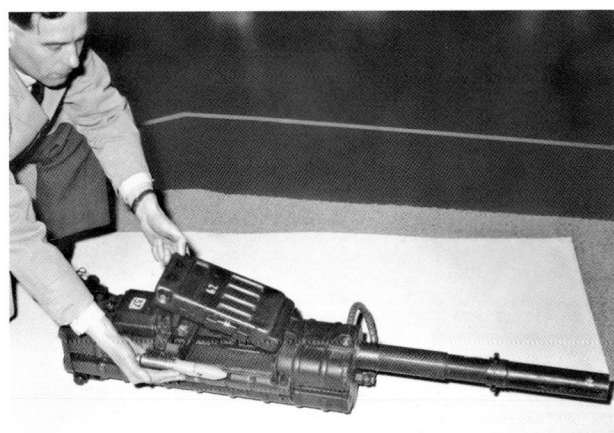

Above:
Developed exclusively for air-to-air combat and weighing a mere 60kg, a single MK 108 cannon could be mounted within the Fw 190's outer wing sections thus eliminating the drag created by externally mounted weapons. The MK 108 could fire a highly destructive thin-walled 30mm projectile known as Minengeschoss (literally mine shell or shot), a round that carried a higher proportion of explosive than standard rounds due to the shell's thinner casing. Minengeschoss provided German fighter pilots with a potent anti-bomber round, its explosive effect being further enhanced when magnesium or aluminium powder was added to the explosive compound. (Chris Goss)

MK 108

Weighing just 60kg with one mounted *within* each outer wing section, the Fw 190's 30mm MK 108 cannon was developed exclusively for air-to-air combat in which the weapon's relatively low muzzle velocity did not overly hamper pilots except to say they had to get closer to score. The MK 108 could use a highly destructive thin-walled projectile known as *Minengeschoss* (originally developed for and used in 20mm weapons) that carried a much higher proportion of explosive than did 'standard' rounds due to the shell's thinner casing.

Above:
Close-up view of the wing armament fitted to Fw 190V5, W/Nr 530765, TG+AT, which became the prototype Fw 190A-6/R2. Extensively tested at the Erprobungsstellen (experimental station) at Tarnewitz, Boltenhagen on the Baltic Sea coast (one of four Luftwaffe test establishments run by Rechlin) during 1943, it shows a 30mm MK 108 cannon in the outboard wing position where it replaced the 20mm MG 151/20. In its Fw 190A-8/R2 form, the wing-mounted 30mm MK 108 was widely used by the Sturmgruppen against USAAF heavy bomber formations. The MK 108 was relatively small and compact and sat slightly below the wing centreline. The circular opening on the leading edge of the wing between the two cannon is a BSK 16 gun camera port. Other points of interest include the retention of the inboard undercarriage doors, the hook under the wing to which gun packs were fitted, and the Peil G VI D/F loop under the rear fuselage. (Chris Goss)

The marriage of the MK 108 with a 330gm (11.6oz) 30mm *Minengeschoss* round provided German fighter pilots with a potent anti-bomber round, the potency of which was further enhanced when magnesium or aluminium powder was added to the explosive compound. (The same round was also used by other MK 103-equipped fighters.)

A German study of downed Allied aircraft revealed that hits from just two, three or four of these rounds were sufficient to shoot down a heavy bomber while just one was often sufficient to down a fighter. It also confirmed that the destructive effect of a high-explosive *M-Schoss* round was much more effective against such targets than an armour-piercing/explosive round because, unless the latter hit a section of armour plate or something similarly solid, it could travel clean through and exit the target without detonating.

MK 108: basic data. *Calibre = 30mm (1.18in); Weight = 60kg (132lb); Cyclic rate = 650 rpm; Length (oa) 1,050mm (41.3in)*

As a footnote, post-war criticism tends to refute the potency of Minengeschoss *rounds given that their thinner casings would, undeniably, yield a reduced fragmentation effect. It would seem, however, that the Luftwaffe was more than satisfied with their explosive effect alone given the lethal damage just two or three of these rounds might inflict within the confines of an aeroplane. Whatever the argument, Nazi Germany didn't invent the concept: thin-walled high-explosive shells (shot) have been familiar to the military for over two centuries, and their modern equivalents remain in use today.*

Left:
Aftermath of an attack by an Fw 190. This image clearly illustrates the power of a 20mm cannon shell after it struck the tail section of a USAAF Martin B-26 Marauder. (NARA)

Appendix 1: Fw 190 gun installations

Fw 190 by type and sub-type	Machine guns	Cannon		Comments
Fw 190 V1 (D-OPZE)	Nil	Nil		Unarmed prototype
Fw 190 V2 (FL+OZ)	2 x MG 17 7.92mm	Nil		1 x MG 17 in each wing root
Fw 190 V5, V5k, V5g	See comment	Nil		Gun installation uncertain but did include 2 x MG 17 in engine cowling
Fw 190A-0	6 x MG 17 7.92mm	Nil		2 x MG 17 in engine cowling: 2 x MG 17 in wing roots plus two in outer wing panels
Fw 190A-0/U1	4 x MG 17 7.92mm	Nil		2 x MG 17 in engine cowling: 2 x MG 17 in wing roots
Fw 190A-0/U2	2 x MG 17 7.92mm 2 x MG 131 13mm	Nil		2 x MG131 in wing roots: 2 x MG 17 in engine cowling
Fw 190A-0/U5 & /U8	2 x MG 17 7.92mm	2 x MG 151/20	20mm	2 x MG 151 in wing roots: 2 x MG 17 in engine cowling
Fw 190A-0/U4/U7/U9 /U10/U11/U12/U13	4 x MG 17 7.92mm	2 x MG FF	20mm	2 x MG 17 in engine cowling: 2 x MG 17 in wing roots; 2 x MG-FF in outer wing panels
Fw 190A-1 (standard A-1 series armament)	4 x MG 17 7.92mm	2 x MG-FF	20mm	2 x MG 17 in engine cowling: 2 x MG 17 in wing roots; 2 x MG-FF in outer wing panels
Fw 190A-2 (standard A-2 series armament)	2 x MG 17 7.92mm	2 x MG 151/20 2 x MG-FF	20mm 20mm	2 x MG 151 in wing roots: 2 x MG-FF in outer wing panels; 2 x MG 17 in engine cowling
Fw 190A-2/U3/U4	2 x MG 17 7.92mm	2 x MG 151/20	20mm	MG-FF removed from U3 (fighter-bomber) and U4 (tactical reconnaissance) variants
Fw 190A-3 (standard A-3 series armament)	2 x MG 17 7.92mm	2 x MG 151/20 2 x MG-FF	20mm 20mm	2 x MG 151 in wing roots: 2 x MG-FF in outer wing panels; 2 x MG 17 in engine cowling
Fw 190A-3/U2/U3/U4	2 x MG 17 7.92mm	2 x MG 151/20	20mm	MG-FF removed
Fw 190A-3/U7	Nil	2 x MG 151/20	20mm	High-altitude fighter variant
Fw 190A-4 (standard A-4 series armament)	2 x MG 17 7.92mm	2 x MG 151/20 2 x MG-FF	20mm 20mm	2 x MG 151 in wing roots: 2 x MG-FF in outer wing panels; 2 x MG 17 in engine cowling
Fw 190A-4/R1/R6/U1/U3/U4/U8	2 x MG 17 7.92mm	2 x MG 151/20	20mm	MG-FF removed. MG 17 deleted on R6 & U8 (optional for U1,U4). U3 rec'd 4 x MG 151
Fw 190A-5 (standard A-5 series armament)	2 x MG 17 7.92mm	2 x MG 151/20 2 x MG-FF	20mm 20mm	2 x MG 151 in wing roots: 2 x MG-FF in outer wing panels; 2 x MG 17 in engine cowling
Fw 190A-5/U2/U3/U8/U9/U13/U14/U15	Nil (except /U1)	2 x MG 151/20 See comments	20mm	MG-FF removed, but U9 could carry 2 x MK 108 30mm cannon or 2 x MG 151/20 in lieu
Fw 190A-5/U10	Nil	4 x MG 151/20	20mm	In wing roots and outer wing panels
Fw 190A-5/U11	Nil	2 x MG 151/20 2 x MK 103	20mm 30mm	MK 103 mounted externally beneath outer wing panels
Fw 190A-5/U12	Nil	6 x MG 151/20	20mm	2 x MG 151 in wing roots: two further pairs in external packs beneath outer wing panels
Fw 190A-6 (standard A-6 series armament)	2 x MG 17 7.92mm	4 x MG 151/20	20mm	In wing roots and outer wing panels: outer pair could be replaced by MG-FF if required
Fw 190A-6/R1	2 x MG 17 7.92mm	6 x MG 151/20	20mm	2 x MG 151 in wing roots: two further pairs in external packs beneath outer wings
Fw 190A-6/R2	2 x MG 17 7.92mm	2 x MG 151/20 2 x MK 108	20mm 30mm	MK 108 mounted in outer wing panels

Appendix 1: Fw 190 gun installations

Fw 190 by type and sub-type	Machine guns	Cannon		Comments
Fw 190A-6/R3	2 x MG 17 7.92mm	2 x MG 151/20 2 x MK 103	20mm 30mm	MK 103 mounted externally beneath outer wing panels
Fw 190A-6/R4	2 x MG 17 7.92mm	4 x MG 151/20	20mm	In wing roots and outer wing panels
Fw 190A-6/R6/N	2 x MG 17 7.92mm	2 x MG 151/20	20mm	No outer wing guns fitted
Fw 190A-7 (standard A-7 series armament)	2 x MG 131 13mm	4 x MG 151/20	20mm	MG 131 in engine cowling. Cannon in wing roots and outer wing panels
Fw 190A-7/R1	2 x MG 131 13mm	6 x MG 151/20	20mm	2 x MG 151 in wing roots: two further pairs in external packs beneath outer wings
Fw 190A-7/R2/R3	2 x MG 131 13mm	2 x MG 151/20 2 x 30mm cannon	20mm	R2 fitted with 2 x MK 108 in outer wing panel. R3 fitted with 2 x MK 103 external gun packs
Fw 190A-8 (standard A-8 series armament)	2 x MG 131 13mm	4 x MG 151/20	20mm	In wing roots and outer wing panels
Fw 190A-8/U1	2 x MG 131 13mm	2 x MG 151/20	20mm	No guns in outer wing panels
Fw 190A-8/R1	2 x MG 131 13mm	6 x MG 151/20	20mm	2 x MG 151 in wing roots: two further pairs in external packs beneath outer wings
Fw 190A-8/R2	2 x MG 131 13mm	2 x MG 151/20 2 x MK 108	20mm 30mm	2 x MK 108 in outer wing panels
Fw 190A-8/R3	?	2 x MG 151/20 2 x MK 103	20mm 30mm	2 x MG 151 in wing roots. 2 x MK 103 beneath outer wing panels
Fw 190A-8/R8	Nil	2 x MG 151/20 2 x MK 108	20mm 30mm	2 x MG 151 in wing roots. MK 108 mounted within outer wing panels
Fw 190A-8/R11/R12	2 x MG 131 13mm	2 x MG 151/20 2 x MK 108	20mm 30mm	2 x MG 151 in wing roots. MK 108 mounted within outer wing panels
Fw 190A-9 (standard A-9 series armament)	2 x MG 131 13mm	4 x MG 151/20	20mm	MG 131 in engine cowling. Cannon in wing roots and outer wing panels
Fw 190A-9/R1	2 x MG 131 13mm	6 x MG 151/20	20mm	2 x MG 151 in wing roots: two further pairs in external packs beneath outer wings
Fw 190A-9/R2/R12	2 x MG 131 13mm	2 x MG 151/20 2 x MK 108	20mm 30mm	MK 108 mounted within outer wing panels
Fw 190A-9/R3/R8	2 x MG 131 13mm	2 x MG 151/20 2 x MK 103	20mm 30mm	MK 103 mounted externally beneath outer wing panels
Fw 190F-1 fighter-bomber	2 x MG 17 7.92mm	2 x MG 151/20	20mm	MG 17 in engine cowling: MG 151/20 in wing roots.
Fw 190F-2 fighter-bomber	2 x MG 17 7.92mm	2 x MG 151/20	20mm	MG 17 in engine cowling: MG 151/20 in wing roots
Fw 190F-3; F-4; F-5 fighter-bombers	2 x MG 17 7.92mm	2 x MG 151/20	20mm	MG 17 in cowling: MG 151/20 in wing roots.
Fw 190F-8 fighter-bomber	2 x MG 131 13mm	2 x MG 151/20	20mm	MG 131 in cowling: MG 151/20 in wing roots. F-8/R-3 variants carried 2 x MK 103 externally
Fw 190F-8/R16	Nil	2 x MG 151/20	20mm	MG 151/20 in wing roots
Fw 190F-8/U1/U2	*MG 131 optional*	2 x MG 151/20	20mm	MG 151/20 in wing roots
Fw 190F-9 fighter-bomber	2 x MG 131 13mm	2 x MG 151/20	20mm	MG 131 in cowling: MG 151/20 in wing roots. F-9/R-3 variants carried 2 x MK 103 externally
Fw 190G-1; G-2; G-3; G-6 fighter-bomber	Nil	2 x MG 151/20	20mm	MG 151/20 in wing roots

Appendix 2: Factory conversion sets

Umrüstbausätz

Umrüstbausätz were modifications to an airframe undertaken on the production line. Identified by the suffix '/U' 'followed by a number after the aircraft sub-type, they generally denoted engine or airframe upgrades such as equipment or armament variations which would be difficult to fit in the field.

Not all *Umrüstbausätz* (factory conversion sets) were applied to the Fw 190, but the main ones included:

•/U3. The fitting of an ETC 501 centreline bomb rack mounted in a long streamlined ventral fairing under the fuselage which could carry up to 500kg (1,100lb) of bombs or a 300-litre (65.9 gal) drop tank. Generally, the outer wing armament was deleted just leaving the cowling 7.92mm MG 17s and the wing root 20mm MG 151 cannon. Initially applied to Fw 190A-3s, (creating the Fw 190A-3/U3, effectively the first of the Fw 190 *Jabos* (*Jagdbombers* – fighter bombers), although some earlier Fw 190A-2s were also retrofitted with the ETC 501 bomb racks (Fw 190A-2/U3) – both types being able to carry a 250kg (550lb) or 500kg bomb, or four 50kg (110lb) bombs on an ER 4 adaptor.
Example: Fw 190A-3/U3

•/U4. Introduced for the dedicated fighter-reconnaissance role, it was fitted with two Rb 12.4 cameras in the rear fuselage and an EK 16 or Robot II gun camera. The /U4 was armed with cowling 7.92mm MG 17s and wing root 20mm MG 151 cannon, but no outer wing guns.
Example: Fw 190A4/U4

•/U7. A small number of Fw 190A-4s were tested as high-altitude fighters with GM1 nitrous oxide power boost which could increase the power of the engine by 300hp for several minutes. Under the designation Fw 190A-4/U7, the aircraft could be identified by the larger compressor air intakes on either side of the cowling. Despite having a reduced overall weight, the normal performance of the aircraft was reduced. Armed with only two wing root mounted 20mm MG 151 cannon.

•/U8. A pair of 300-litre drop tanks, one under each wing, carried on VTr Ju 87 racks, with duralumin fairings produced by Weserflug, plus a centreline ETC 501 bomb rack. The outer wing-mounted cannon and 7.92mm MG 17s were removed to save weight.
Examples: Fw 190A-4/U8, a *Jabo-Rei* (*Jagdbomber Reichweite* – long-range fighter-bomber). The A-4/U8 was the precursor of the Fw 190G-1.
The Fw 190A-5/U8 was another *Jabo-Rei*, fitted with under-wing 300-litre drop tanks and a centreline ETC 501 bomb rack. Only two wing root MG 151s were fitted. It was later re-designated Fw 190G-2.

•/U11 and /U12. Created for dedicated bomber attack variants. While generally retaining the cowling 7.92mm MG 17s and wing root 20mm MG 151s, the outer wing 20mm MG FF cannon were replaced by underwing gun pod fairings – the /U11 with a single 30mm MK 103 in each fairing, and the /U12 with a WB 151 (Waffen-Behälter 151/20) cannon pod under each wing fitted with a pair of 20mm MG151/20 cannon.
Example: Fw 190A-5/U12

Note: The Fw 190A-3/U1 and Fw 190A-3/U2 were single experimental Fw 190s – the /U1 (W.Nr 130270) was the first Fw 190 to have the engine mount extended by 15cm (6 inches), which was later standardised on the production Fw 190A-5 model. The /U2 (W.Nr 130386) had RZ 65 73mm rocket launcher racks fitted under the wings with three rockets per wing. Production-wise, the Fw 190A-5/U2 was designed as a night *Jabo-Rei* and featured anti-reflective fittings and exhaust flame dampers. A centre-line ETC 501 rack typically held a 250kg bomb, and wing-mounted racks mounted 300ltr drop tanks. An EK16 gun camera, as well as landing lights, were fitted to the wing leading edges. The /U2 was armed with only two 20mm MG 151 cannon.

Rüstsätz (Auxiliary apparatus/ field kits)

Rüstsätz modification kits, identified by the suffix '/R' designation, were packaged in kit form, usually by the aircraft manufacturer, and were designed to be fitted in the field, as opposed to *Umrüstbausätz* modifications which were typically fitted on the production line. However, this was not a hard and fast rule, as during production runs various *Rüstsätz* kits were often fitted by factories in order to meet Luftwaffe demands. An '/R' designation was also occasionally applied to more complex changes in an aircraft's airframe design that were much more suitably completed at production line facilities.

Typically, *Rüstsätz* kits would include extra cannon or machine gun armament, (most often mounted in underwing gun pods), bomb and drop tank fittings, extra armour, fuel, and various electrical system upgrades. Some of these upgrades would become almost standard on certain Fw 190 sub-types.

The *Rüstsätz* modification kits most associated with the Fw 190 were:

- /R1. The first of this new series of easier-to-install field kits was the /R1, produced in 1943. Initially fitted to the Fw 190A-4 (creating the Fw 190A-4/R1), it comprised a FuG 16ZY radio set with a Morane 'whip' aerial fitted under the port wing. These aircraft, called *Leitjäger* (Fighter Formation Leaders), could be tracked and directed from the ground via special R/T equipment called *Y-Verfahren* (Y-Control). More frequent use of this equipment was made from the Fw 190A-5 onwards, with the standard radio equipment upgraded to the FuG 16ZE and the fitting of a WB 151 twin 20mm cannon pod under each wing.
Examples: Fw 190A-6/R1, Fw 190A-7/R1 and Fw 190A-8/R1

- /R2: Fitting a 30mm MK 108 cannon in the outer wing positions replacing the original 20mm MG FF cannon
Examples: Fw 190A-6/R2, Fw 190A-7/R2, Fw 190A-8/R2 and Fw 190A-9/R2

- /R3: Fitting of two 30mm MK 103 cannon pods, one under each wing. The original outer wing 20mm MG FF cannon being removed.
Examples: Fw 190A-6/R3 *Fw 190A-7/R3*, Fw 190A-8/R3, *Fw 190A-9/R3*

- /R4: A GM1 nitrous oxide boost was fitted to the standard BMW 801D/Q engine. A GM1 injection increased power for short amounts of up to 10 minutes at a time.
Example: Fw 190-6/R4 and Fw 190A-8/R4.

- /R5: Additional 115-liitre (25.2 gallon) fuel tank in fuselage.
Example: Fw 190A-8/R5.

- /R6: Fitting of *Werfer-Granate* 21 (W.Gr 21) rocket tubes, one mid-span under each wing .
Examples: Fw 190A-4/R6, Fw 190A-5/R6, Fw 190A-6/R6, Fw 190A-7/R6 and Fw 190A-8/R6.

- /R7: Addition of various thickness appliqué armour plating to the forward fuselage and cockpit sides.
Examples: Fw 190A-6/R7, Fw 190A-7/R7 and Fw 190A-8/R7.

- /R8: A combination of the R2 (replacement of wing mounted 20mm MG FF cannon with 30mm MK 108 cannon) and R7 (addition of 5mm appliqué armour plating to the cockpit sides and 30mm canopy and windscreen armoured glass) on the *Rammjäger* (ram fighter) and *Sturmbock* (battering ram) dedicated bomber attack variants.
Examples: Fw 190A-8/R8 and Fw 190A-9/R8.

- /R11: Fitting of a FuG 125 radio, a PKS 12 radio direction finder, and heated windscreen to create a *Shlechtwetterjäger* (all-weather fighter).
Examples: Fw 190A-8/R11 and Fw 190A-9/R11. Also, the Fw 190A-5/R11 – a night fighter conversion fitted with FuG 217 Neptun (Neptune) radar equipment with three dipole antenna mounted vertically fore and aft of the cockpit and above and below the wings. Anti-glare shields were fitted over the exhaust louvres.

- /R12: A combination of the R2 (replacement of wing mounted 20mm MG FF cannon with 30mm MK 108 cannon) and R11 FuG 125 radio, PKS 12 radio direction finder, and heated windscreen to create a *Shlechtwetterjäger* (all-weather fighter), plus anti-glare shields over the exhaust louvres and flame dampers on the cannon barrels.
Example: Fw 190A-8/R12

Glossary of terms and abbreviations

Luftwaffe flying unit structure

Geschwader: The basic Luftwaffe tactical operational unit that was broadly equivalent to an RAF Group. *Geschwader* (plural) were defined by the roles for which their aircraft were designed, and their crews trained for. For example:
Jagdgeschwader (JG): Fighter Group
Kampfgeschwader (KG): Bomber Group (literally Battle Group)
Zerstörergeschwader (ZG): Heavy twin-engined/long-range Fighter Group (literally Destroyer Group) ***Stukageschwader*** (StG): Dive Bomber Group, etc.

In the spring and summer of 1941, when the Fw 190 first entered Luftwaffe service a *Jagdgeschwader* typically consisted of three **Gruppen**, each broadly equivalent to an RAF Wing, which in turn were made up of three **Staffeln** (roughly equivalent to an RAF Squadron). However, some *Jagdgeschwadern*, added a fourth **Staffel** within some of its *Gruppen*, which caused some re-adjustments in the *Staffel* numbering procedure, (see below). Occasionally, a fourth *Gruppe* was added to a Geschwader.

Each **Gruppe** had a **Stabsschwarm** (Staff Flight), generally of four or so aircraft, which included the *Gruppen Kommandeur*, and usually the unit Adjutant and Technical Officer, who were generally pilots. However, not all members of the *Gruppe* staff were necessarily pilots, and often non-staff rank pilots, including experienced NCOs flew with the *Stabsschwarm*.

The *Geschwader* also had a *Stabsschwarm*, the **Geschwaderstab**, led by the *Geschwader Kommodore*, which invariably consisted of four or so aircraft and generally included the *Geschwader* Adjutant and *Geschwader* Technical Officer plus experienced pilots; again, they could be drawn from any of the *Staffeln* within the *Geschwader*.

With some twelve to sixteen aircraft in a fully up-to-strength *Staffel*, the total strength of an average *Jagdgeschwader* could have been anything been between 100 to 150 or so aircraft, including the *Stabsschwarm* – at least on paper. Actual operational strength varied considerably, and the average serviceable figure would have been somewhat lower, especially as the war progressed.

Aircraft unit markings in brief
Jagdgeschwader single-engined fighters including the Fw 190, were invariably identified by coloured numerals, generally positioned in front of the fuselage *balkenkreuze* (crosses) on both sides. These numerals were in *Staffel* colours, often outlined in a contrasting colour.
White for the first *Staffeln* within a *Gruppe*;
Red (or black) for the second *Staffeln* within a *Gruppe*;
Yellow (or brown) for the third *Staffeln* within a *Gruppe*.
(When a fourth *Gruppe* was added to a *Geschwader*, the individual *Staffeln* were often allowed to devise their own identification system albeit roughly based on the standard system.)

To the rear of the fuselage *balkenkreuze*, there appeared a system of bars, wavy lines, discs or crosses which identified the *Gruppe* within the *Geschwader*.
I Gruppe aircraft had nothing behind the fuselage *balkenkreuze*;
II Gruppe aircraft generally had a horizontal bar behind the fuselage *balkenkreuze*;
III Gruppe had a vertical bar or a wavy horizontal bar behind the fuselage *balkenkreuze*, while…
IV Gruppe aircraft often had a disc or a small cross behind the fuselage *balkenkreuze*.

When written down for administrative purposes, *Staffeln* were numbered in Arabic numerals while *Gruppen* were numbered in roman numerals, for example:
1./JG 26 = 1 Staffel, (I Gruppe) of JG 26
II./JG 26 = II Gruppe of JG 26 (which comprised of 4, 5 and 6 Staffeln)

Both *Geschwader* and *Gruppe Stab* machines sported a system of chevrons and bars in the same place as the *Staffel* numerals, generally placed in front of the fuselage *balkenreuze*.
When written down, Stab III/JG 26 = III Gruppe Stab.

In-Flight formations
Luftwaffe fighter pilots employed a loose section of two aircraft, **Rotte** (pair), based on a leader called the **Rottenführer**

(pair leader) followed at a distance of about 180 metres (200 yards) by his wingman (nicknamed *Rottenhund* or *Katschmarek*), who also flew slightly higher and stayed with his leader at all times. While the leader was free to search for enemy aircraft and concentrate on achieving 'kills', his wingman concentrated on searching the airspace in the leader's blind spots, behind and below. Any attacking aircraft could be sandwiched between the two fighters. Two **Rotten** usually teamed up to create a four aircraft **Schwärm** in which all the pilots could watch the area of space around them. Two or three *Schwarme* made up a *Staffel*.

Specialised units

Specialised units, such as **Jabo** (Jagd Bomber – Fighter Bomber), or **SchnellKampfGeschwarder** (SKG – Fast Bomber (Battle) Group), often employed their own identification systems, frequently using coloured letters rather than numerals, or different colour combinations of numerals.

Sturmbock	literally 'battering ram'
Sturmjäger	bomber-destroyer
Wilde Sau	Wild Boar

Luftwaffe – RAF comparative ranks

Oberst (Colonel)	Group Captain
Oberstleutnant (Lieutenant Colonel)	Wing Commander
Major	Squadron Leader
Hauptman (Hptm) (Captain)	Flight Lieutenant
Oberleutnant (Oblt)	Flying Officer
Leutnant	Pilot Officer
Oberfähnrich	[no RAF equivalent]
Stabsfeldwebel	Warrant officer
Oberfeldwebel (Ofw)	Flight Sergeant
Feldwebel (Fw)	Sergeant
Unterfeldwebel	[no RAF equivalent]
Unteroffizier (Uffz)	Corporal
Obergefrieter	Senior Aircraftsman

Supplementary list of general terms

Balkenkreuze	Luftwaffe national cross (marking)
Einsatzstaffel	independent test squadron
Erprobungskommando	operational test unit
Erprobungsstaffel	operational trials squadron
Erprobungsstelle der Luftwaffe	Test Centre of the Air Force
Erprobungsstellen	experimental station
grosse fläche	large wing
Gruppenkommandeur	wing commander (position – not a rank)
Hakenkreuze	swastika
Jagdbomber (Jabo)	fighter bombers
Jagdfliegerschule	fighter pilot school
Jabo-Rei (*Jagdbomber mit vergrosserter Reichweite*)	extended range fighter-bomber
kleine fläche	small wing
Kommandogerät	'brain box'
Reichsluftfahrtministerium (RLM)	Reich Air Ministry
Reichsverteidigung	Defence of the Reich bands/*Geschwader* identification bands
Schlachtgeschwader	ground attack wing
Staffelkapitän	squadron commander (position – not a rank)
Staffelkapitäne	squadron commanders (plural)
stammkennzeichen	factory code
TO	Technical Officer
Werf Granat (WGr)	literally 'stove pipe' (fired time-fuzed explosive shells into bomber formations)

Gun camera images

Left:
Although poor quality, this gun camera image shows an Fw 190 being attacked from the rear by Major Walter G Beckham, USAAF, flying a Republic P-47 Thunderbolt of the 351st FS, 353rd FG, on 11th November 1943. (NARA)

Below:
These four gun camera images show the demise of another Fw 190. Taken over France by a USAAF fighter circa May 1944, it shows the Fw 190 descending to tree-top height in an attempt to shake off its pursuer and then, hit by .5 calibre bullets, it explodes in a blinding flash, and then in a flaming ball of smoke and debris, plunges the few remaining feet to earth. (NARA)